THIS BOOK IS A GIFT
FROM
THE CHRISTOPHER AWARDS
2003

TO
LACORDAIRE ACADEMY
ELEMENTARY

The Amazing Beginning of You

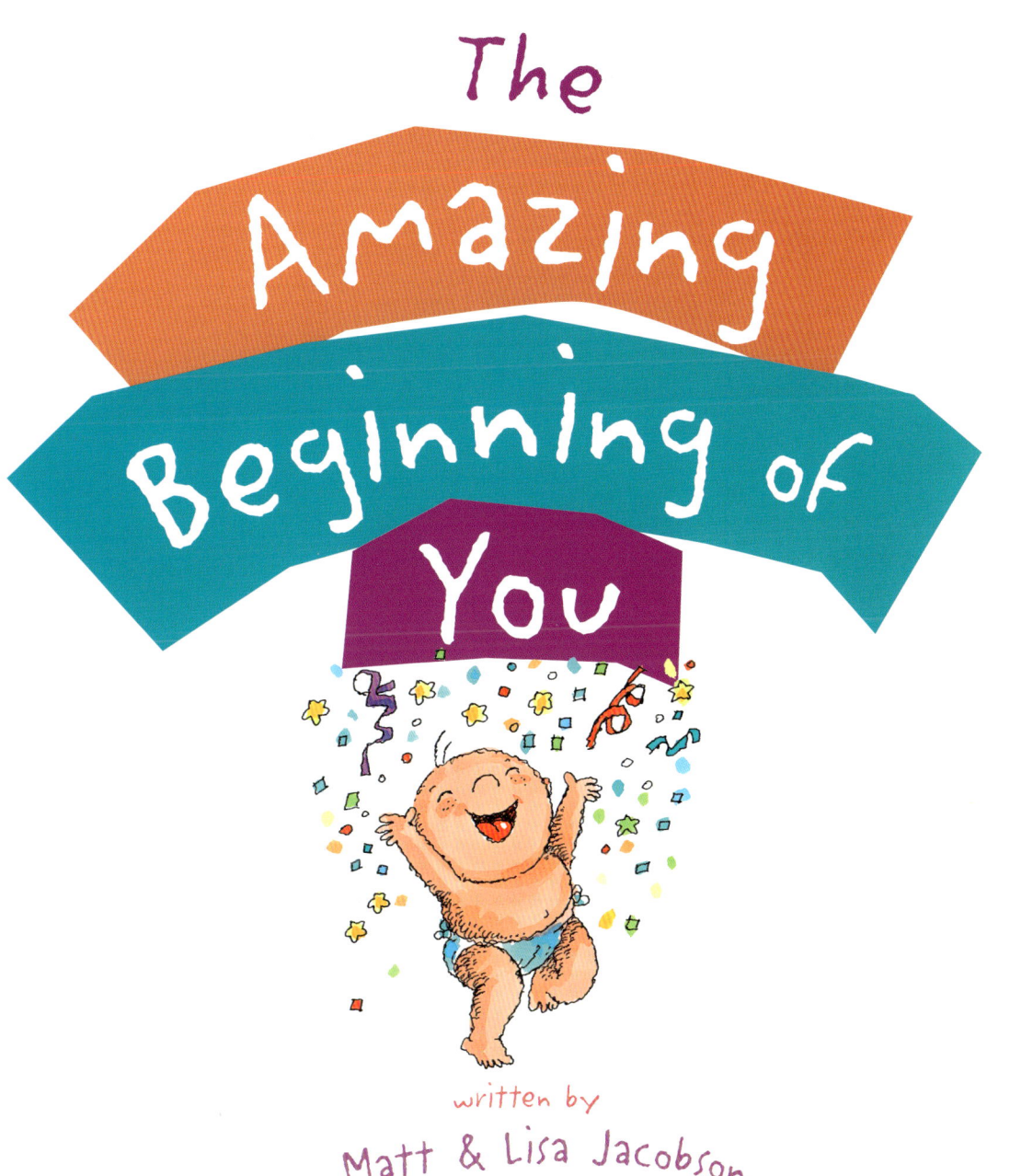

written by
Matt & Lisa Jacobson

illustrated by
Jared Lee

Zonderkidz

Zonder**kidz**™
The children's group of Zondervan

www.zonderkidz.com

The Amazing Beginning of You
ISBN: 0-310-702178

Copyright © 2002 by Matt and Lisa Jacobson
Illustrations © 2002 by Jared Lee
Photos on pages 12, 22, 23, 24, 25, 28, 31, 32 and front cover by Lennart Nilsson/Albert Bonniers Förlag AD, A CHILD IS BORN, Dell Publishing Co. Photos on page 10 by David M. Phillips/Photo Researchers, Inc. Photos on page 14 by David M. Phillips/Photo Researchers, Inc., Petit Format/Science Source/Photo Researchers, Inc., Studio/Science Photo Library/Photo Researchers, Inc., and Omikron/Photo Researchers, Inc. Photo on page 16 by Petit Format/Science Source/Photo Researchers, Inc. Photo on page 20 by Petit Format/Nestle/Science Source/Photo Researchers, Inc. Photo on page 26 by Neil Bromhall/Genesis Films/Science Photo Library/Photo Researchers, Inc. Photo on page 27 by Neil Bromhall/Science Photo Library/Photo Researchers, Inc. Photo on page 29 by Petit Format/Nestle/Science Source/Photo Researchers, Inc. Photos on pages 15, 16, 18, and 19 by Synergy Photographic. Photo on page 8 by Paul Kuroda/Superstock. Photo on page 19 and back cover © by Science Pictures Limited/CORBIS. Photos on page 30 by Photodisc. Photo on page 33 by Eyewire. Photos on page 34 by Camille Tokerud Photography Inc./International Stock and Owen Fraken/CORBIS. Sonogram on page 31 by 3-D Babygram.

Requests for information should be addressed to:
Zonderkidz, Grand Rapids, Michigan 49530

All Scripture quotations, unless otherwise indicated, are taken from Holy Bible: New International Reader's Version [NirV]. Copyright © 1995, 1996 by International Bible Society. Used by permission of Zondervan. All rights reserved. No part of this publication may be reproduced, stored in a retrieval system, or transmitted in any form or by any means—electronic, mechanical, photocopy, recording, or any other—except for brief quotations in printed reviews, without the prior permission of the publisher.

Zonderkidz is a trademark of Zondervan.

Editor: Gwen Ellis
Art Direction and Design: Jody Langley

Printed in China
02 03 04 05/HK/5 4 3 2 1

This book is dedicated to children and young people everywhere with the hope that they will understand their Divine origin.

— M.J. & L.J.

An Amazing Story

When we tell someone our life's story, we usually start with the day we were born. But that's not really the beginning. Have you ever thought about that? Your life actually began a long time before you were born. In fact, your life started about nine months before you were born . . . before you arrived and said,

"Hey, Mom, how 'bout some milk?"

I'm sure you've already done some interesting things in life. But did you know that you did some truly *amazing* things before you were born? Well, you did, and that's what we are going to explore in this book.

So what was it like inside Mom's tummy . . . from the very beginning? It seems kind of odd that as big as you are today, you came from inside your mom, doesn't it? But that's where you got your start in life. Just keep reading, and we'll take a look at the awesome story of your life—before you were born.

For you created my inmost being; you knit me together in my mother's womb. I praise you because I am fearfully and wonderfully made; your works are wonderful, I know that full well. My frame was not hidden from you when I was made in the secret place. When I was woven together in the depths of the earth, your eyes saw my unformed body. All the days ordained for me were written in your book before one of them came to be.

Psalm 139: 13-16

How You Got Started!

You were one-of-a-kind right from the start—a real special kid. You were God's idea. God picked out the exact day that you would come into the world. He had a plan for you from the very beginning. His plan started with your dad and mom. ∿ Inside her body, your mom had about 400 ovum which are cells that develop into eggs. These eggs are released one at a time each month. When you came into being, God chose the ovum from which you grew. Isn't that amazing? Out of four hundred ovum, God selected the one that became you. He handpicked you even before you were born. ∿ Once your ovum was selected, there was no time to lose. Your egg would last for twenty-four hours—only one day. Something had to happen quickly so that you could be complete. ∿ For you to be created, your dad needed to be involved, too. Part of you started with your mom (the egg), and the other part came from your dad. This part from your dad is called the sperm. It took one egg from your mom and one sperm from your dad to complete the beginning of your new life. ∿ A baby does not start to grow every time your mom and dad love each other and have intercourse. It only happens when everything is just right and that's what happened when you started. Then the egg and sperm came together. About 350 million sperm tried to get to the egg first to fertilize it . . . and only one made it. Yours won the race. Your sperm beat all the rest! You were a winner even before you were born! The exact moment your new life started is called conception—the moment the egg and sperm come together.

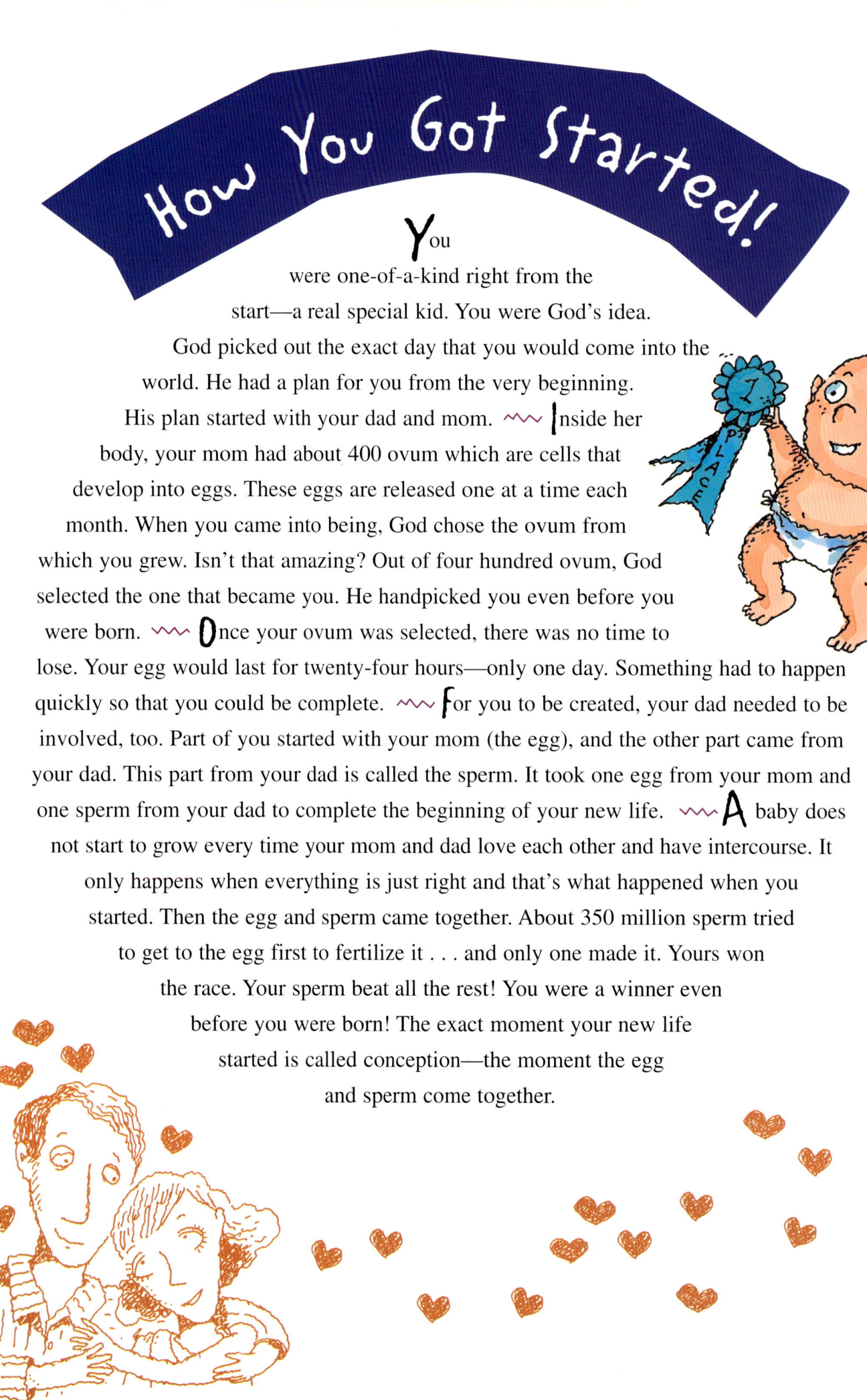

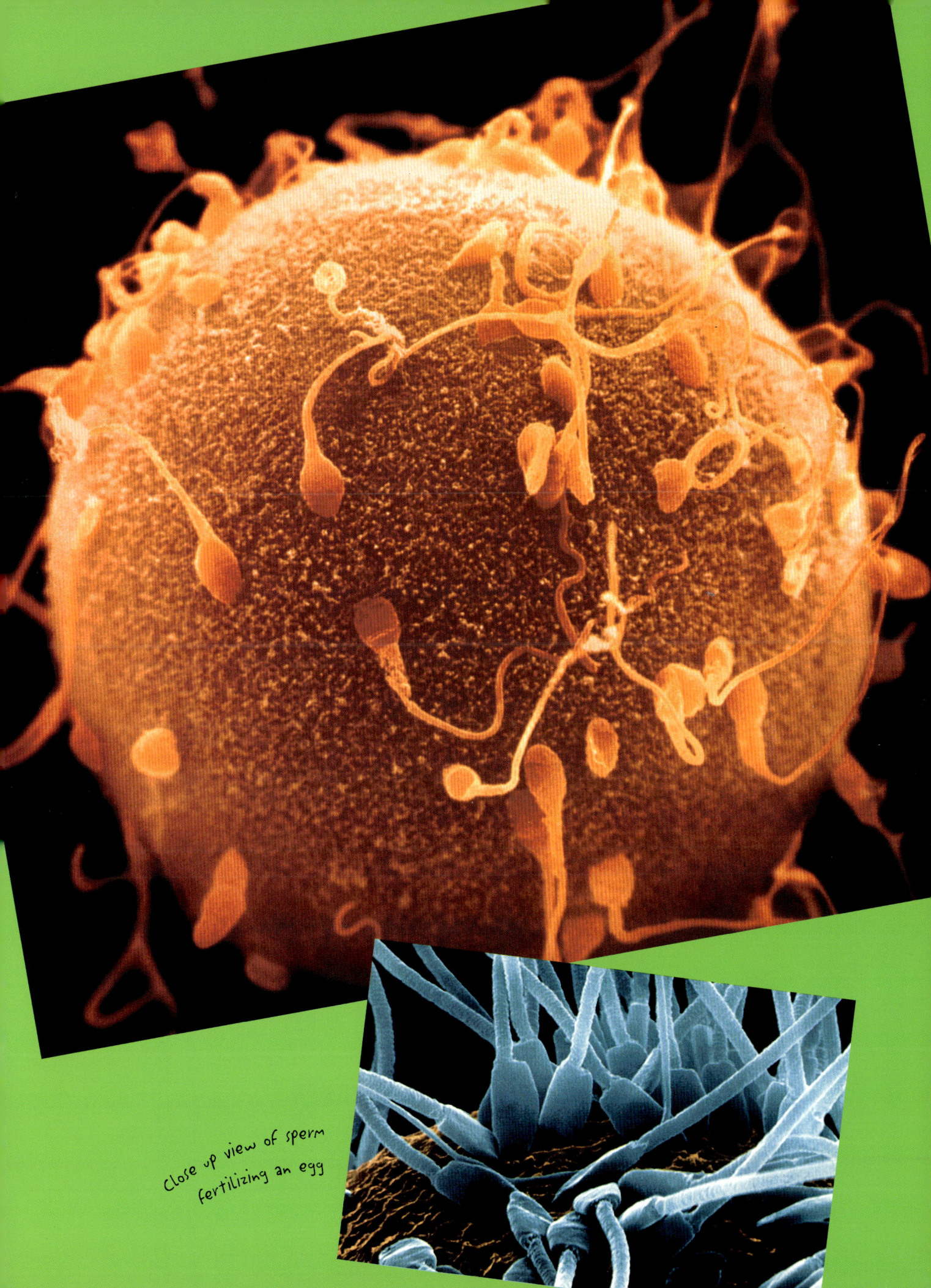

Close up view of sperm fertilizing an egg

a closer look

The egg is developed in the ovary. The two ovaries contain about four hundred ovum (cells that will become eggs). Only one egg is released each month. The egg travels down the fallopian tube, where the sperm meets it. The sperm have been released into the vagina from the male penis in a process called "ejaculation." The sperm then begin their journey to the egg. Most of the sperm die along the way. But all of the sperm that make the journey to the egg try to penetrate it. Only one sperm successfully enters the egg to fertilize it. This is the moment of conception—the moment life begins. After one sperm penetrates the egg, no others can enter. The egg immediately closes its outer membrane to all the other sperm. The miracle of life has begun. The fertilized egg begins to divide every twelve to fifteen hours. While dividing and growing, this group of cells moves through the fallopian tube and into the uterus, where it eventually attaches to the uterus wall. This process takes about five to eight days.

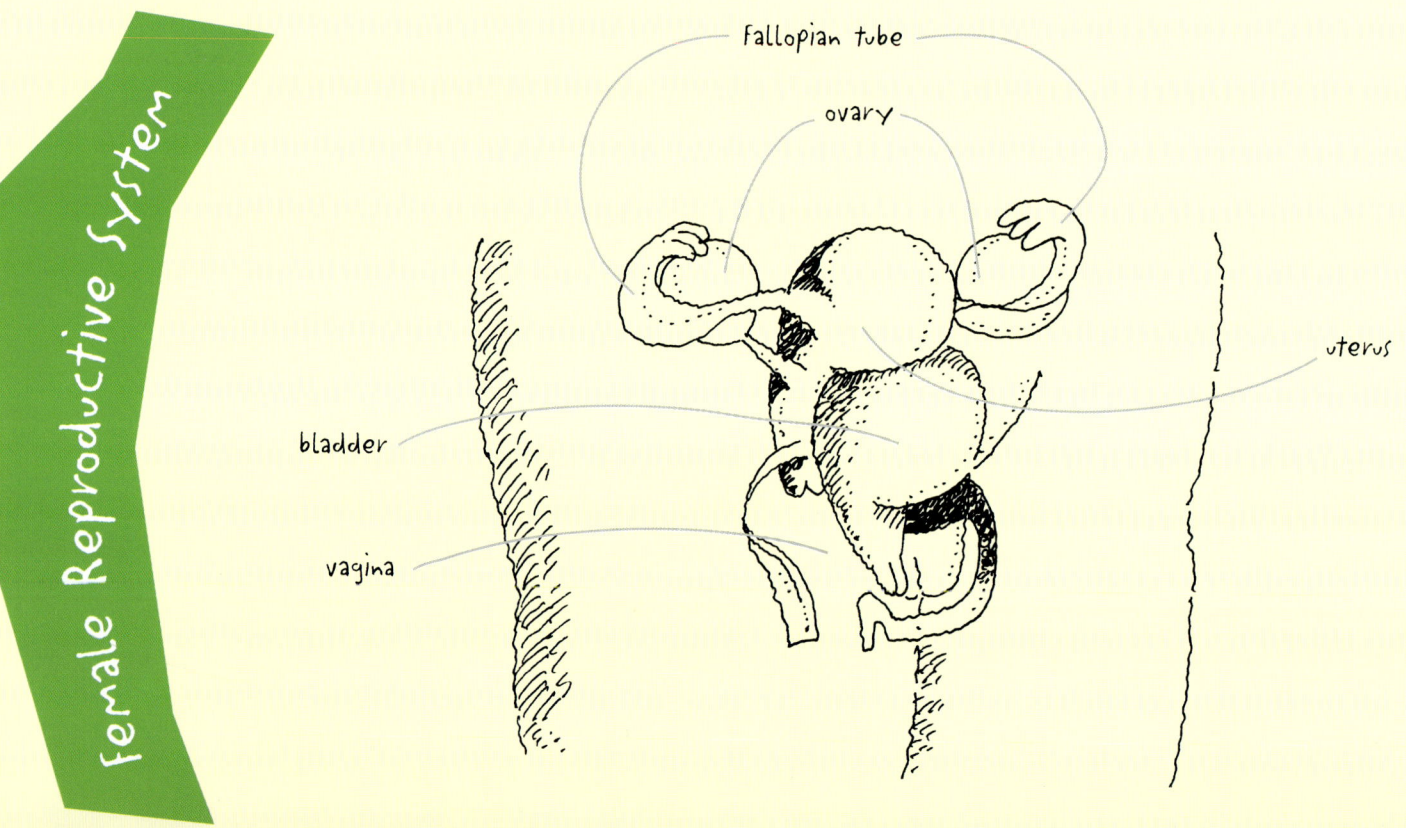

Female Reproductive System

- fallopian tube
- ovary
- uterus
- bladder
- vagina

Careful! The egg is moving slowly through the fallopian tube while the cells begin dividing.

Sometimes after the sperm and the egg join together, the egg splits in two. When this happens, identical twins are born. At other times two eggs and two sperm join at the same time and fraternal twins are born. Identical twins will always be two boys or two girls, but fraternal twins could be two boys that are very different from each other. Or fraternal twins might be one boy and one girl. Twins don't happen very often. They happen in about one out of ninety-five births.

Male Reproductive System

Sperm are produced in the testes (plural for testical). Sperm are constantly produced at the rate of one hundred million every day. In a healthy young male about one thousand sperm are produced each second. When ejaculation occurs, the sperm travel from the male penis through the vagina to the fallopian tube, where one sperm finds and fertilizes the egg. The sperm's journey usually takes several hours.

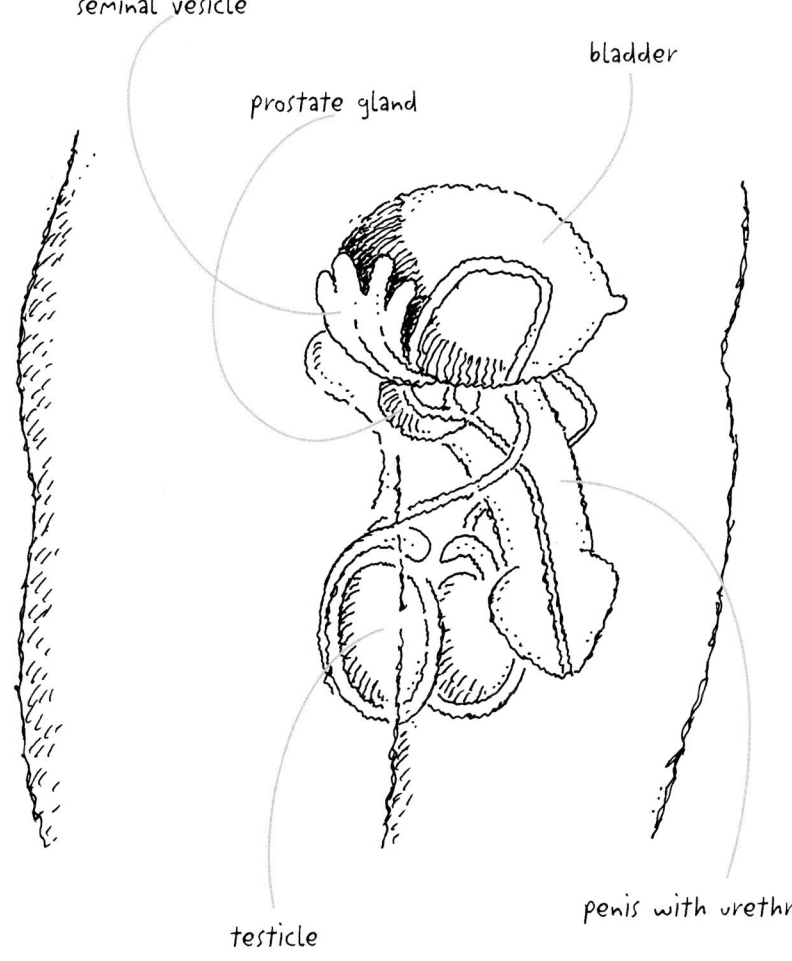

seminal vesicle
prostate gland
bladder
testicle
penis with urethra

month 1 — A Miracle

Once the miracle of life began, you were given a new name. You were then called a "zygote", which is another name for a fertilized egg. Sounds funny, doesn't it? Zygote! Well, you didn't stay a zygote for very long, only about twelve hours. As soon as you started to grow and begin your journey down the fallopian tube, you had another name change and it was as odd as the first one. At this point you were called a "blastocyst". You kept this name while you moved down the fallopian tube and attached to the wall of the uterus. This event is called "implantation". Once implantation occurred, you were no longer a blastocyst. You were then an "embryo". You kept this name for the next eight weeks. Let's take a closer look.

a closer look

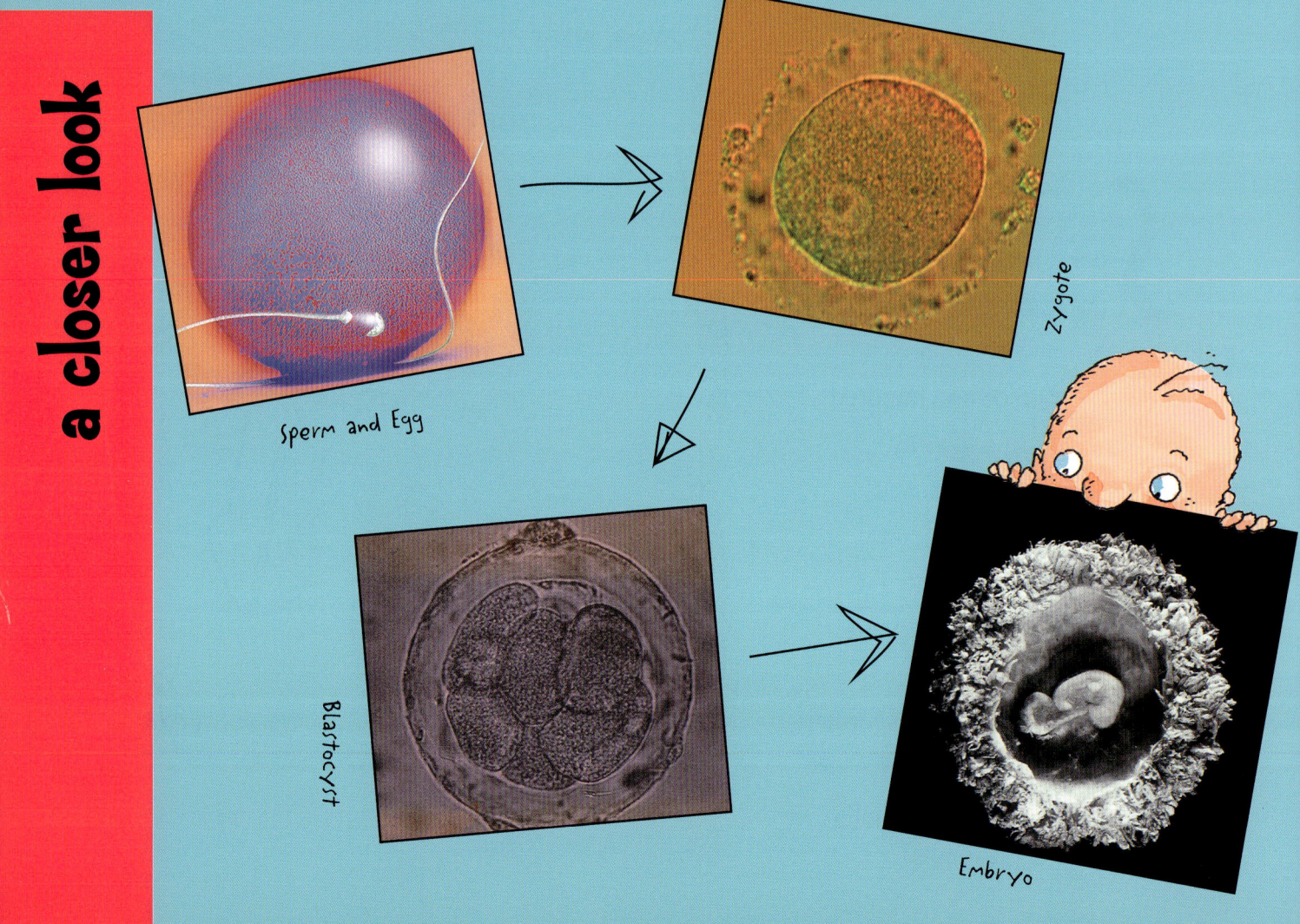

Sperm and Egg

Zygote

Blastocyst

Embryo

The embryo has divided into three main sections:

1. **Top Layer:** the neural tube which is where the brain, spinal cord, nerves, and backbone are.
2. **Middle layer:** heart and circulatory system (blood vessels and arteries).
3. **Lower layer:** lungs, intestines, and urinary system.

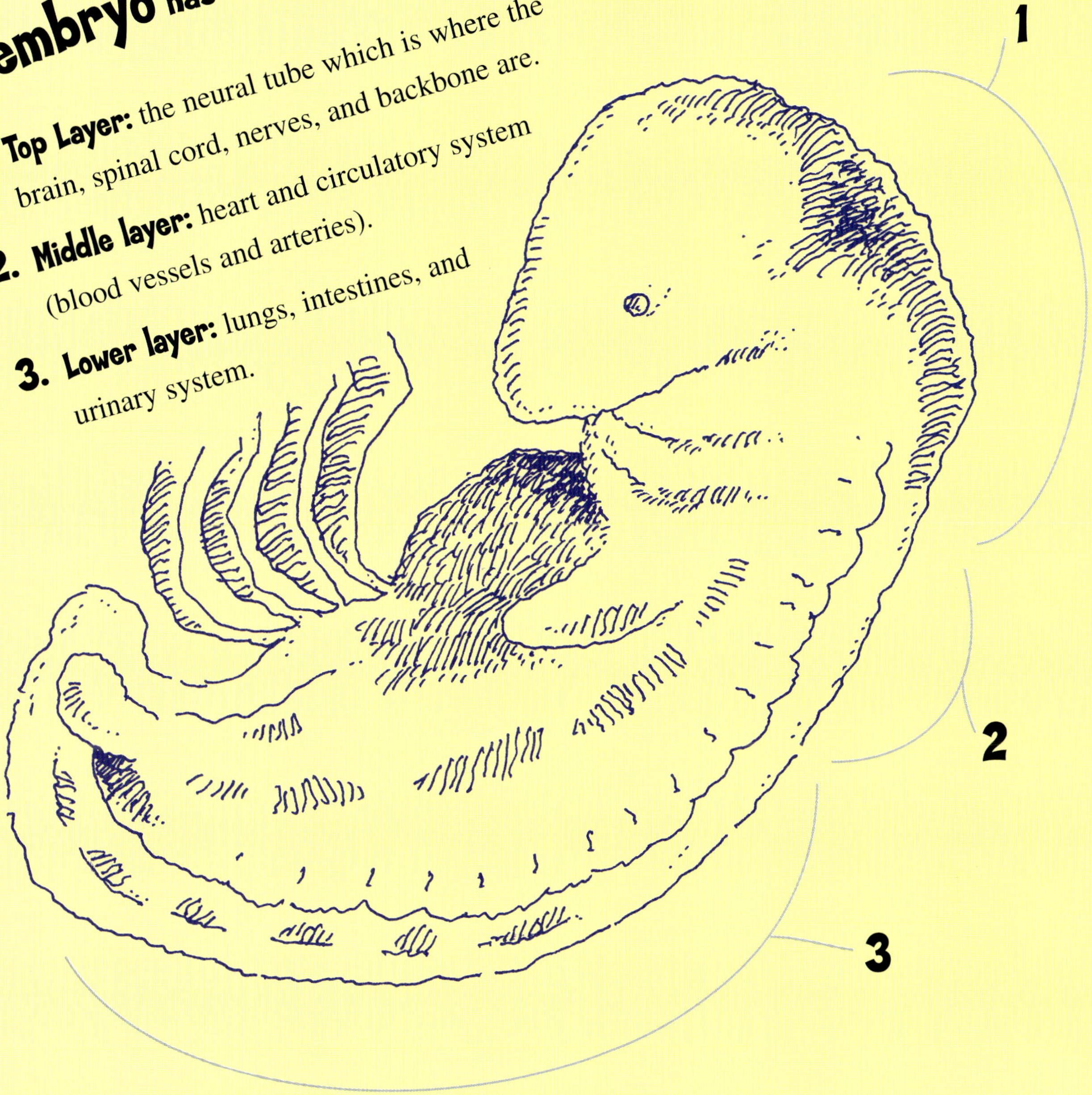

Actual Size!

You're probably wondering just how big you were by now. Well, even though you'd traveled a long way, and had already done some amazing things, at three weeks you were about the size of an apple seed. You still looked a little odd, but it was really you! It wouldn't take long before you got really cute!

a closer look

4 to 5 weeks old

Can you believe you were only the size of an apple seed? And your heart was even smaller—about the size of a poppy seed. But as small as it was, it had already started beating and pumping blood through your tiny, developing body. You were only three weeks old and your heart was beating—now, that's a miracle!

The end of the first month of your life inside your mom had come. Take a look at the fingernail on your little finger—that's right, your pinky. At this time in your new life, you were the size of that fingernail.

Yee-ha!

Right from the moment of conception, each of your cells contained all your genetic information in chromosomes. Chromosomes look like small noodles that cross in the middle. Your chromosomes contained all the information that would determine the way you would develop: what color your eyes would be, whether your hair would be curly or straight, how tall you would be—everything about the way you develop physically was contained in these little pairs of matter. Isn't that awesome! God's plan for you was in place before your egg and sperm came together. He planned who you would be and the kind of person you would become.

WHOA! You were only this big!

month 2 — Your New Home

By now you had grown to the size of a navy bean. (Ask your mom to show you one.) Even someone as small as a navy bean has to eat! So how did you get your breakfast? How did you eat inside Mom's uterus? Sometime around the twelfth day after your egg and sperm came together and you attached to the wall of the uterus, a series of blood vessels began to form. Remember, at this time you were just a little group of cells. The place where you attached to the uterus wall was where these blood vessels formed. Over time the vessels grew into a vast network of passages called the "placenta". This placenta brought food to you and took away waste. ～ **W**here your navel is (some people call it a belly button), before you were born there was a tube that stretched from that spot on your tummy to the wall of the placenta. The tube is called the "umbilical cord". Through the umbilical cord you received nutrients (food) from your mother. ～ **Y**our little heart was working hard; beating at one hundred fifty beats each minute. That's about twice as fast as your mom's heart beats. Your heart was divided into two chambers, one on the right and one on the left. Your blood vessels were easy to see.

a closer look

During this second month a thin pouch, called the "amniotic sac", formed around you. It was like a balloon filled with salty water. That water is called "amniotic fluid". For the next eight months you floated in this fluid, safe inside the amniotic sac. ～ **Y**ou might be wondering how you breathed in all that water. Well, you don't have to breathe. Just as your food was supplied from your mom, you also got all the oxygen you needed the same way, from your mother's blood supply, through the umbilical cord. Your mom was breathing for both of you!

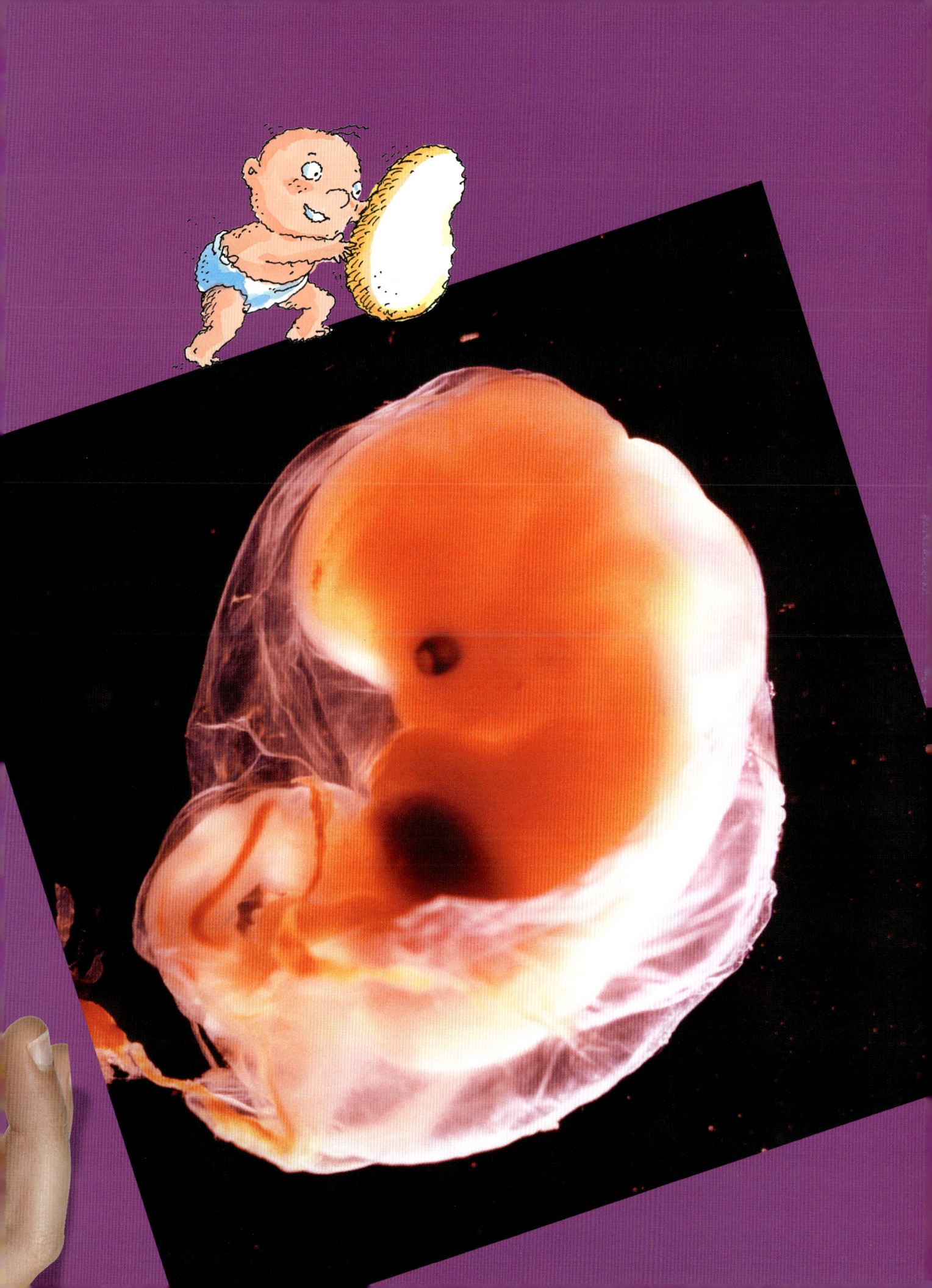

The time was coming for another name change. Do you remember what your name was up until now? You were called an embryo but not for much longer. You were soon to be called a "fetus". If you listen to the news, you often hear people talking about the fetus. Fetus has a special meaning. It is a Latin word that means "little one". Fetus is the name that you were given when you are about eight weeks old.

Your muscles and bones were now starting to form. Your face and neck had developed and, your eyes had color. Your skin was so thin that in many places it was transparent, which means you could see right through it!

Now look closely at one of your fingers. Do you see the curved lines? Those are your fingerprints. Have you heard it said that no two snowflakes are alike? The same is true of fingerprints. No two people have the same fingerprints. No one else in the whole world has fingerprints like yours. You are an original! God only made one of you! By the time you were two months old inside your mom, God had already designed your unique set of fingerprints!

So there you were, only one inch long, but you had hands and feet, and even fingers and toes! Not only that, but everything on the inside was there, too. All your internal organs were now in place. Even though you were a mere two months old and had a lot of growing yet to do, you had all the parts of a fully-grown adult.

Only this big!

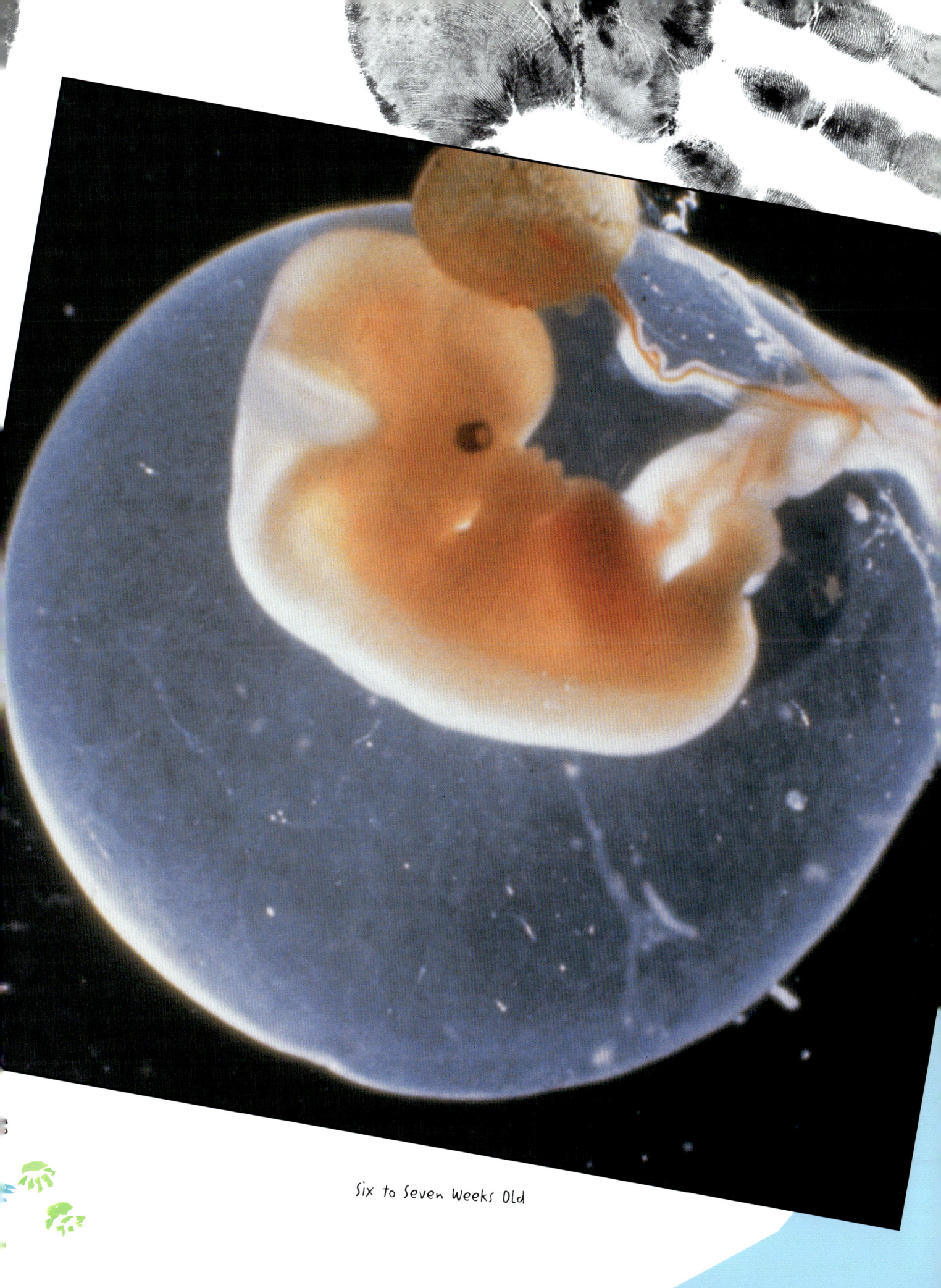

Six to Seven Weeks Old

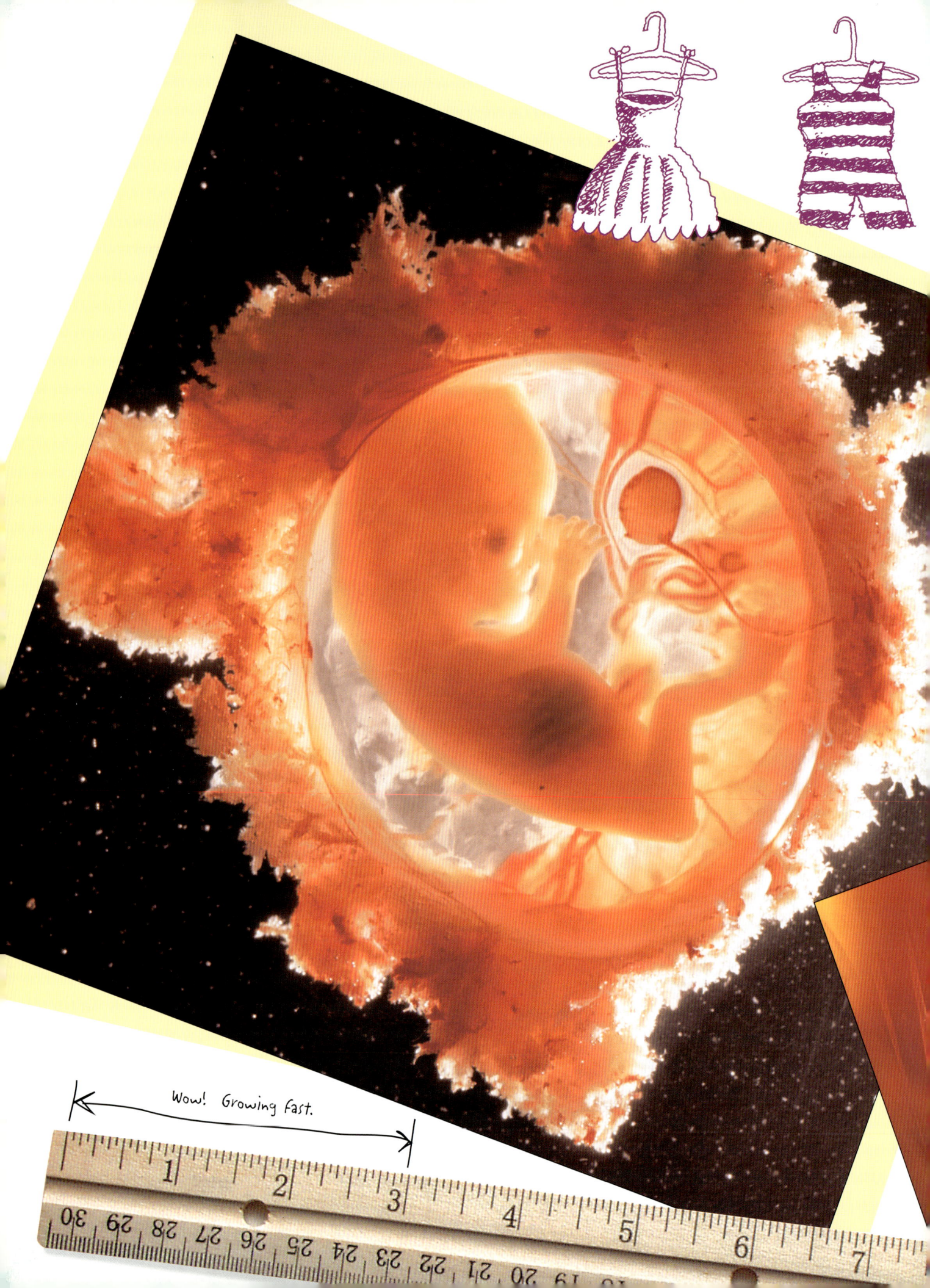

Wow! Growing fast.

month 3
Growing Fast & Strong

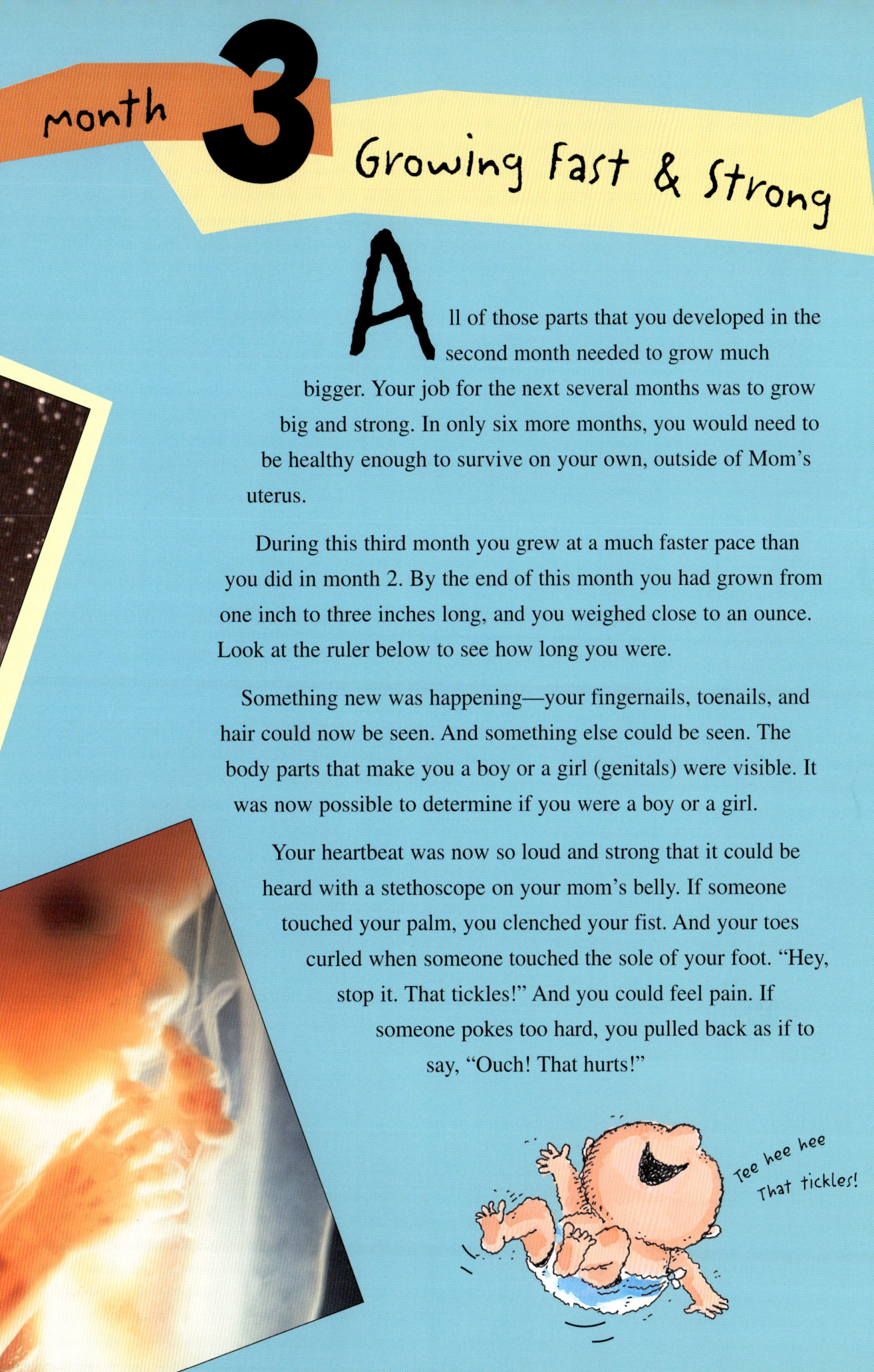

All of those parts that you developed in the second month needed to grow much bigger. Your job for the next several months was to grow big and strong. In only six more months, you would need to be healthy enough to survive on your own, outside of Mom's uterus.

During this third month you grew at a much faster pace than you did in month 2. By the end of this month you had grown from one inch to three inches long, and you weighed close to an ounce. Look at the ruler below to see how long you were.

Something new was happening—your fingernails, toenails, and hair could now be seen. And something else could be seen. The body parts that make you a boy or a girl (genitals) were visible. It was now possible to determine if you were a boy or a girl.

Your heartbeat was now so loud and strong that it could be heard with a stethoscope on your mom's belly. If someone touched your palm, you clenched your fist. And your toes curled when someone touched the sole of your foot. "Hey, stop it. That tickles!" And you could feel pain. If someone pokes too hard, you pulled back as if to say, "Ouch! That hurts!"

Tee hee hee That tickles!

month 4 Learning New Skills

During this fourth month, when someone softly poked your mom's tummy, you opened your mouth as if you wanted some milk! Every time you brought your hand up to your mouth, you started sucking. Why were you doing this now? You started to practice sucking because you would have to suck to eat as soon as you were born. Even though you were getting your food through the umbilical cord, as soon as you were born you would need to drink milk through your mouth. That's why you started to practice now—so you would be ready to drink when you were born.

Do you like to make faces in the mirror? You practiced this a lot during this fourth month, too. You made many different faces. You made an angry face, a sad face, a happy face, and sometimes you squinted as if there were too much light. You also invented a game—it was called pull and squeeze the umbilical cord. You played for hours, practicing your new skills of pulling and squeezing.

Another skill you worked very hard to develop was breathing. Remember, you didn't really need to breathe since your oxygen supply was coming from your mother's blood supply through the umbilical cord. But you started to practice breathing. You took very shallow breaths. You needed to be ready for the day you were born.

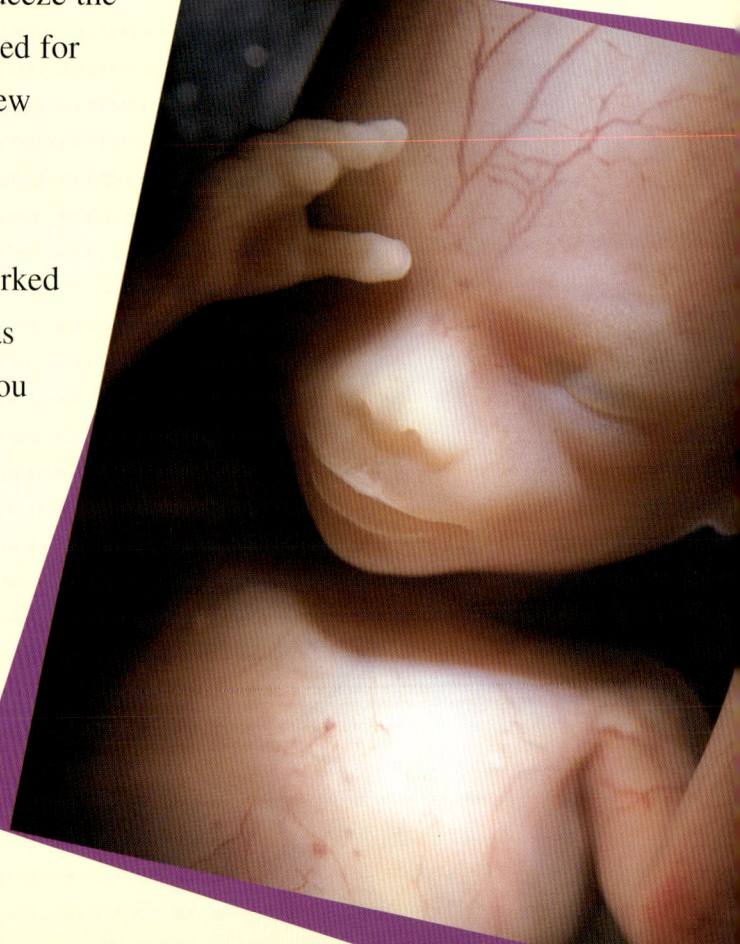

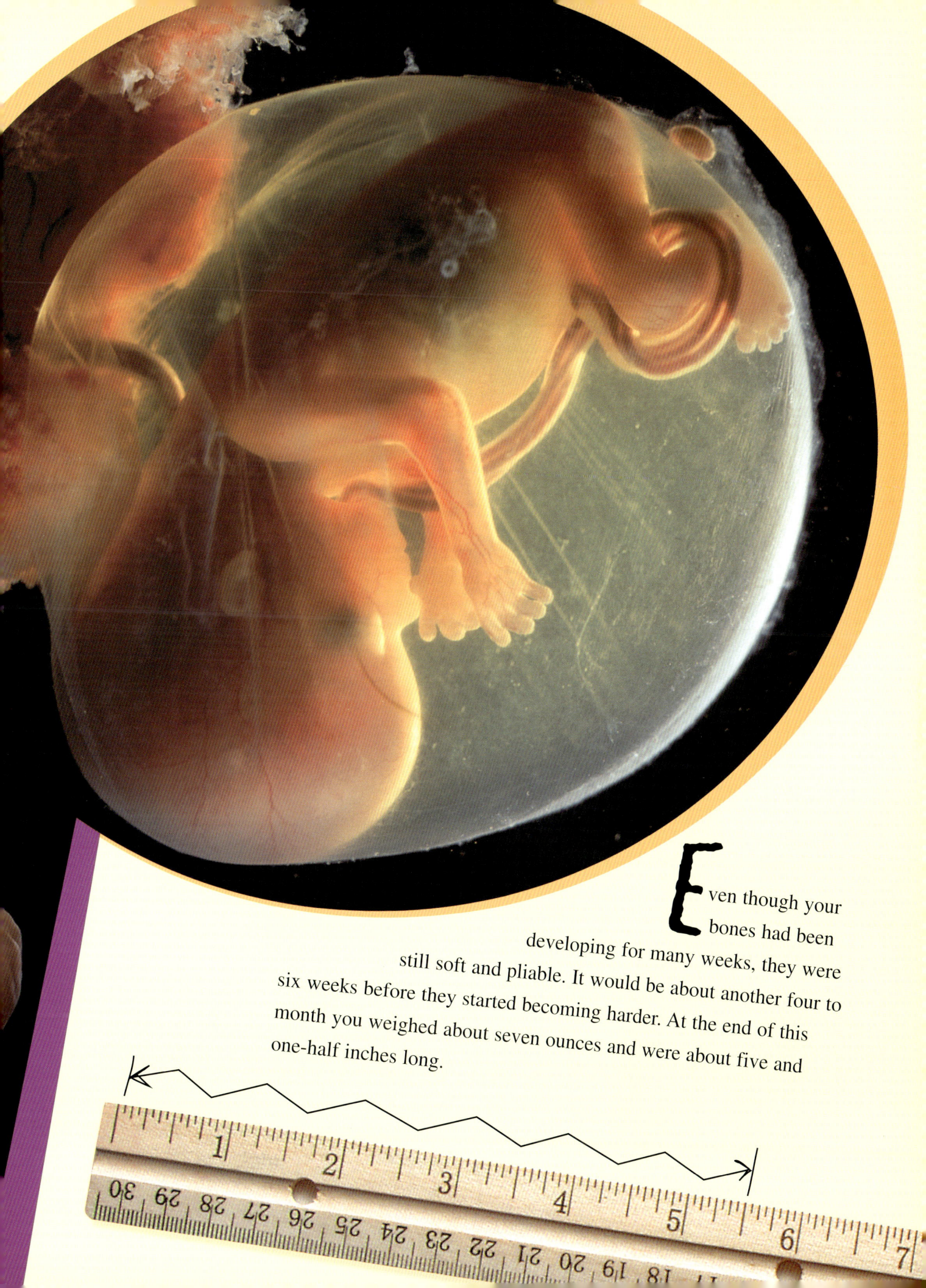

Even though your bones had been developing for many weeks, they were still soft and pliable. It would be about another four to six weeks before they started becoming harder. At the end of this month you weighed about seven ounces and were about five and one-half inches long.

month 5

The World Outside

Even though you'd been moving around like an excited puppy for several weeks, now for the first time your mom could feel you moving around inside her. Inside the watery warmth, you could hear your mother's stomach gurgling and her heart beating rhythmically. And you were very aware of what was happening outside of your mom, too. You could hear all kinds of sounds. By now, you recognized your mother's voice and your dad's, too. If someone played music, or started singing, you listened to the sounds. You especially liked music you'd heard many times.

Have you ever had the hiccups? Before you were born, you hiccupped a lot! And every time you did, your mom felt it. When your mom walked around, rocked in a rocking chair, the gentle movement put you to sleep. But as soon as she lay down to sleep, you woke up and started moving around again!

Have you ever spent all day playing in a swimming pool or in the water at the lake? What do your hands look like when you finally come out of the water? Shriveled like prunes, right? Remember that in mom's uterus you were in the amniotic sac that was filled with amniotic fluid. You were in that water (fluid) all day, every day, for nine months. If your skin had not been protected, you would have looked just like a prune when you were born.

But God thought of everything. He made sure your skin was covered with a creamy white substance. It was almost like the cream your mom might use to soften her hands. It's called vernix, and it protects your skin from being in the amniotic fluid all the time. Some babies are still covered with vernix when they are born. Ask your mom if you were.

Now you're probably wondering, *"If I'd been eating for five months, didn't I have to go to the bathroom somewhere?"* Well, yes . . . and no. You did need to urinate often. And you urinated right into the amniotic fluid that we

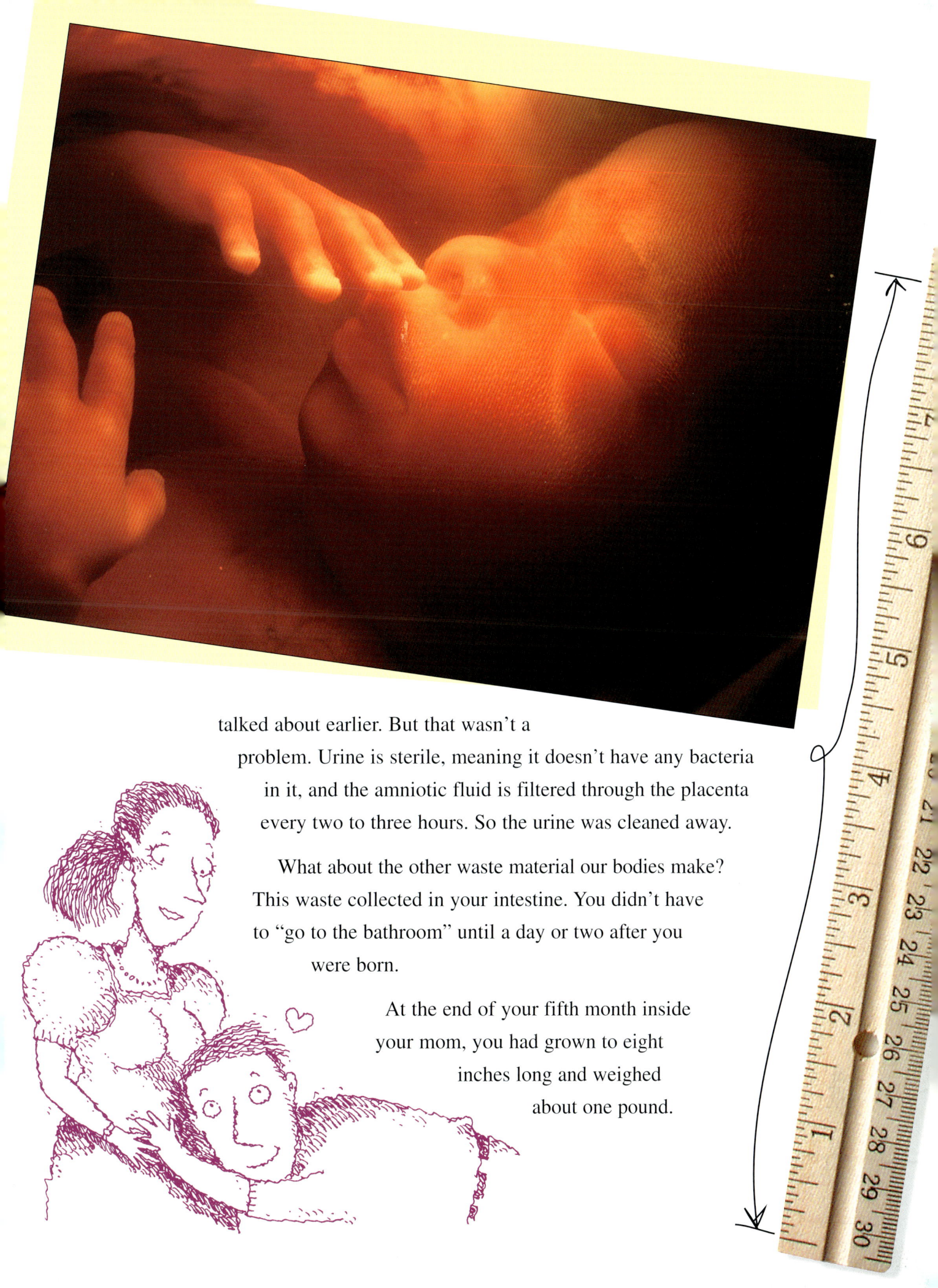

talked about earlier. But that wasn't a problem. Urine is sterile, meaning it doesn't have any bacteria in it, and the amniotic fluid is filtered through the placenta every two to three hours. So the urine was cleaned away.

What about the other waste material our bodies make? This waste collected in your intestine. You didn't have to "go to the bathroom" until a day or two after you were born.

At the end of your fifth month inside your mom, you had grown to eight inches long and weighed about one pound.

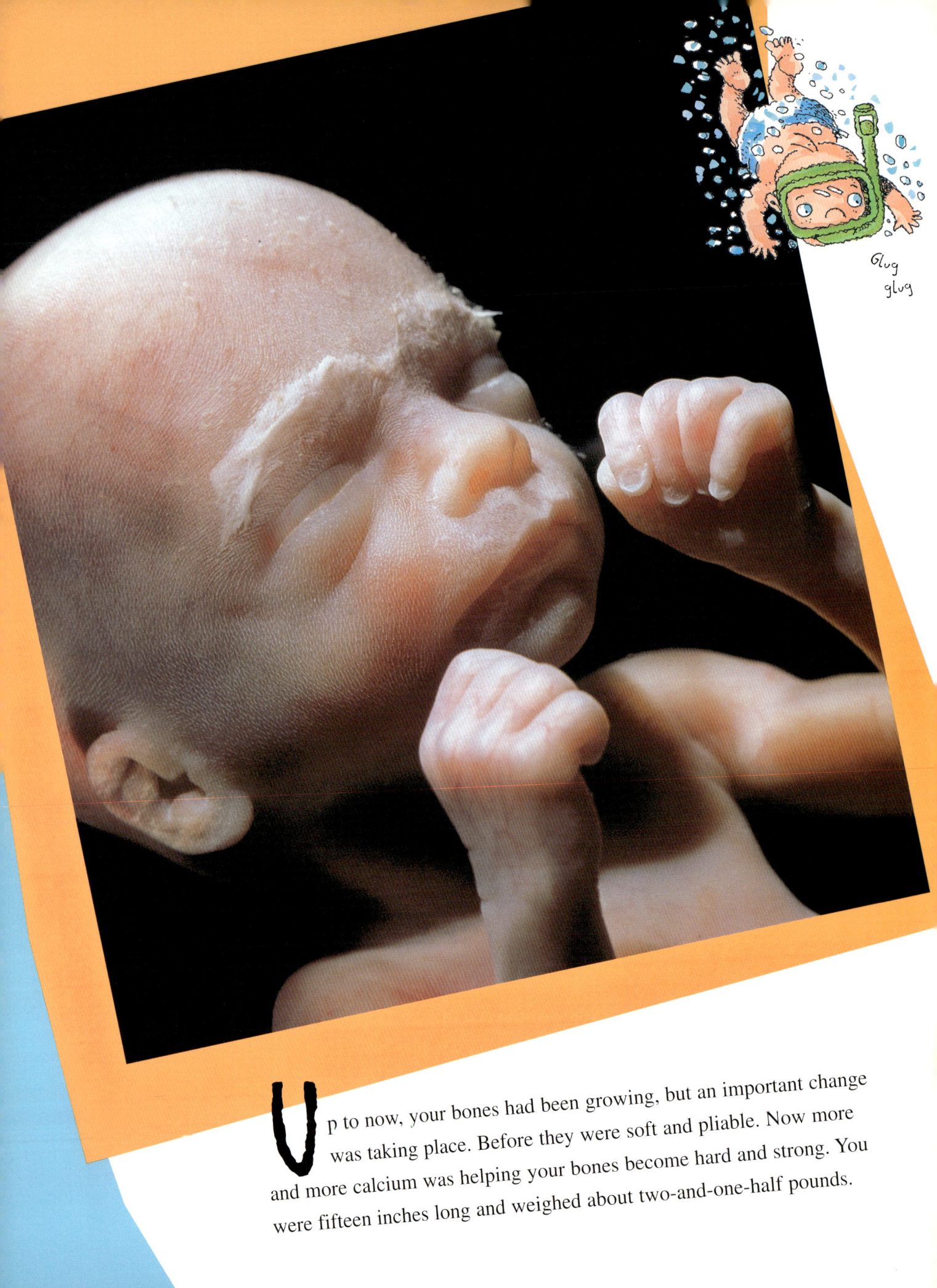

Glug glug

Up to now, your bones had been growing, but an important change was taking place. Before they were soft and pliable. Now more and more calcium was helping your bones become hard and strong. You were fifteen inches long and weighed about two-and-one-half pounds.

month 6 Practice Makes Perfect

You had been inside your mom for six months. In only three more months you would be ready to come out and see the world. But before you could see, you had to open your eyes. Toward the end of this month you began to open your eyes, practicing for the big day when you would see the world for the first time.

You probably don't think much about your lungs. You just breathe without thinking about it. But even so, you couldn't live without breathing. When you were born, you had to start breathing right away because you no longer got oxygen from your mother's blood. You had to get it on your own. That's why everyone is happy when a newborn baby starts to cry. This shows that the baby is breathing.

If you are going to be good at something, you have to practice. If you want to be good at baseball or ice-skating, you have to practice. The same rule applies to breathing. You needed to be good at breathing before you were born . . . so you practiced a lot. Now, you might ask, "If I was in amniotic fluid and I was breathing in, wouldn't I drown?" Yes, you would, except for one thing. Don't forget that you were still getting all your oxygen from your mom's blood supply, through the umbilical cord. So having fluid in your lungs at this point was no problem.

Close up of hands and mouth

month 7 Getting Smarter Every Day

We've talked about your muscles and bones growing. They continued to grow while the rest of your body did some catching up. Until this month your head was large compared with the rest of your body. But by the end of this month your body would catch up with your head.

Even though your head was big, it was during this month that your brain did a lot of growing. And you were using your brain more and more. You were thinking and even dreaming! I wonder what you spent the seventh month dreaming about.

Can you think of any foods that you like a lot because you think they taste so good? To taste something, you need taste buds. During the seventh month your taste buds developed.

You now weighed twice as much as you did in the sixth month. In fact, you had gained about one-half pound every week during this seventh month. Your body was storing fat that you would need for the first few days outside of Mom, when you were learning how to drink milk. By the end of this month you weighed about four pounds and looked like a newborn baby . . . but you were not quite ready to come out yet.

Mmm...good!

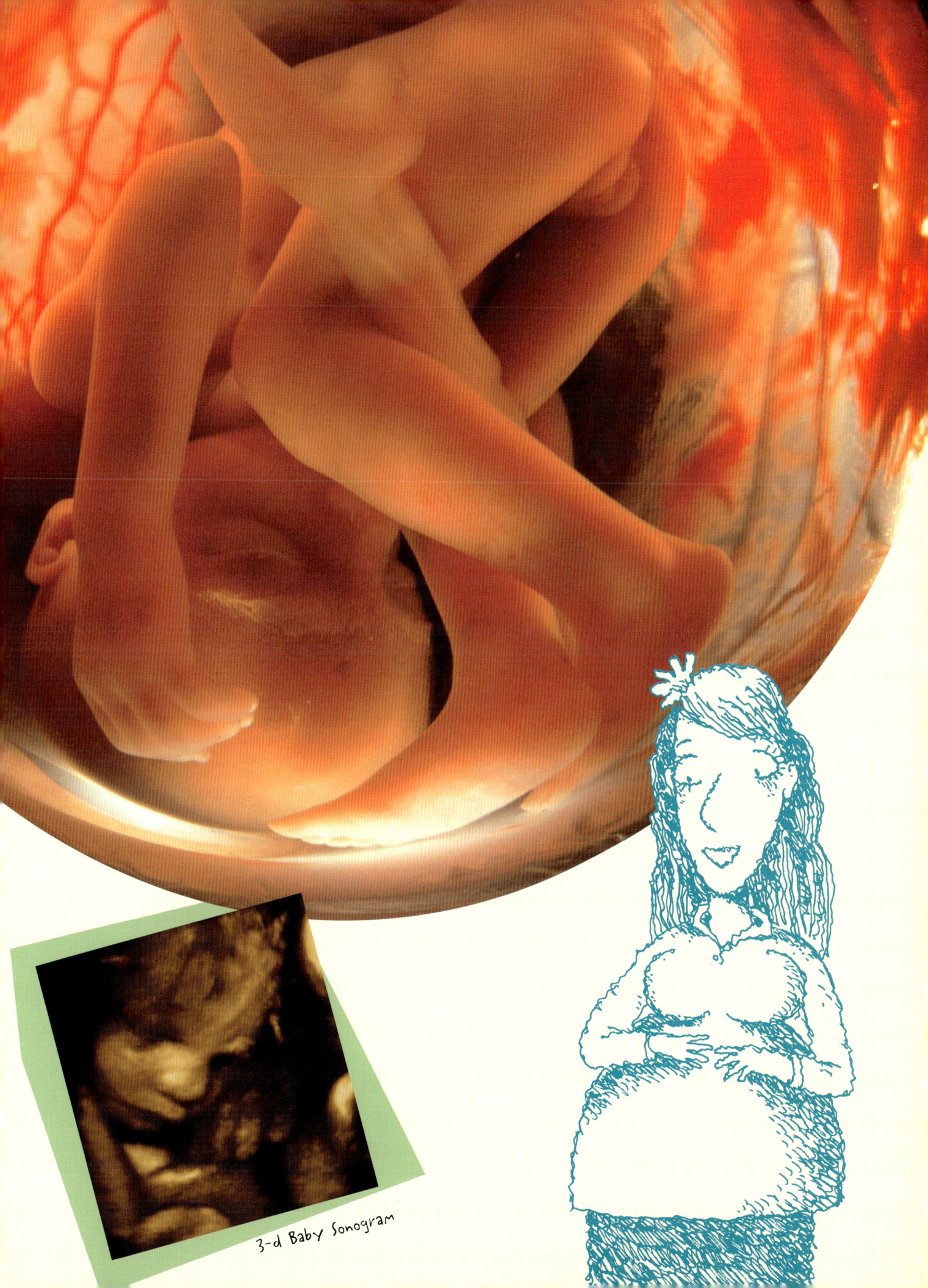
3-d Baby Sonogram

month 8
Running Out of Room

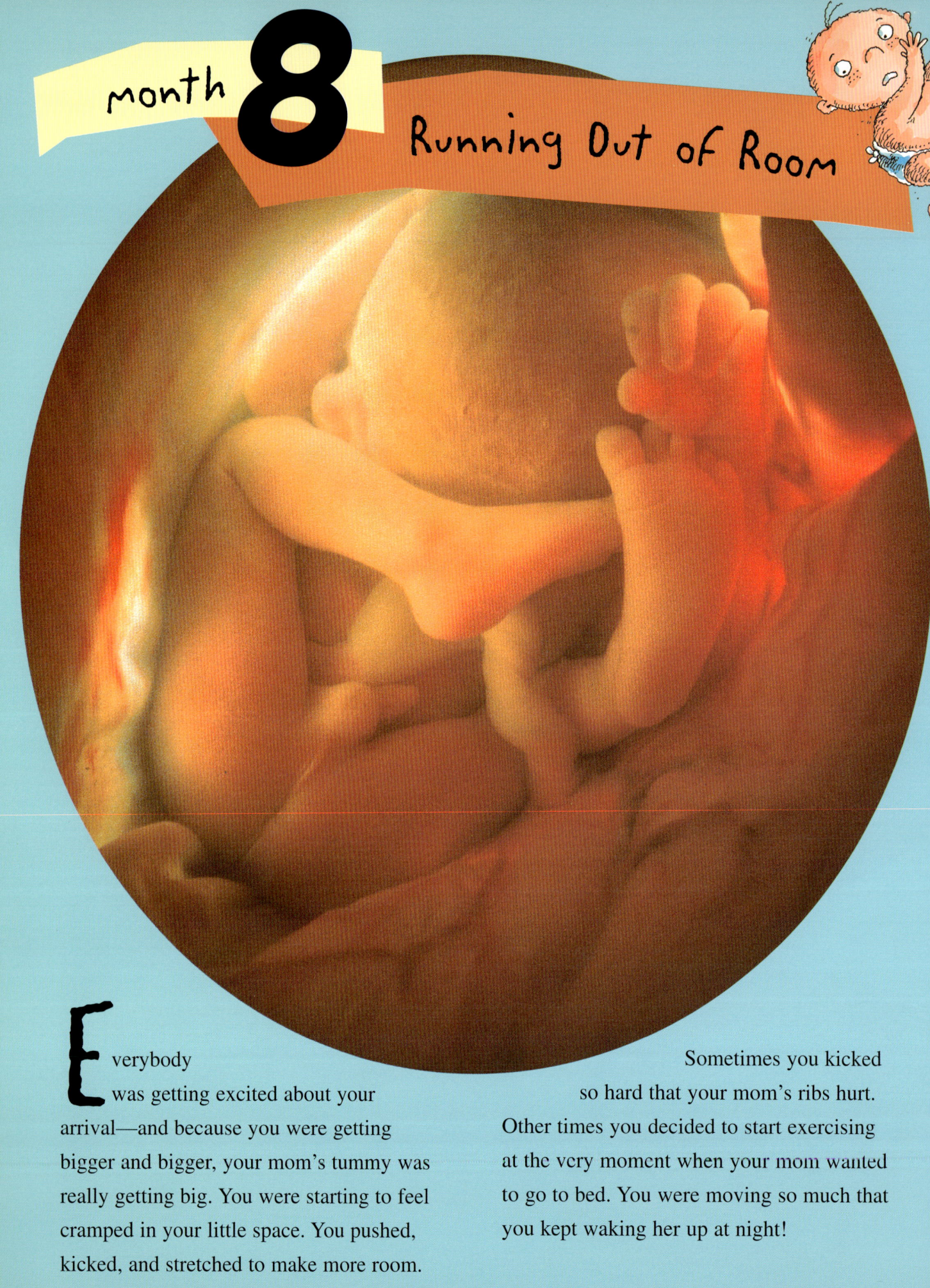

Everybody was getting excited about your arrival—and because you were getting bigger and bigger, your mom's tummy was really getting big. You were starting to feel cramped in your little space. You pushed, kicked, and stretched to make more room.

Sometimes you kicked so hard that your mom's ribs hurt. Other times you decided to start exercising at the very moment when your mom wanted to go to bed. You were moving so much that you kept waking her up at night!

Toward the end of this month you started preparing to come out. Your head turned down, and you started getting into position to come out the birth canal. Some babies forget to turn downward, and if they stay heads up, they are called "breech babies", which means that they will be born feet first.

By now your lungs were fully developed and ready to breathe air. Although babies need to stay inside their mothers for nine months, if you had been born the eighth month, you would have done just fine. You would have been a little small, but you would have been able to breathe and eat and all the other things necessary to life.

Your skull [diagram] is made up of several different bones. When you were inside your mom, and for several months after you came out, these bones remained loosely attached. They could move against each other without coming apart. This was very important because when you were ready to come, you needed to get through the birth canal. If these bones couldn't move, you wouldn't fit through the opening.

pelvic bone

Baby's skull bones

a closer look

From time to time, for various reasons, babies are born before the full nine months. These babies are called "premature". They are a little smaller and require special care to help them along for the first month or two.

month 9
Welcome to the outside World

Birth Canal

You were still gaining weight—about one-half ounce a day, but there was no more room. It was time to come out! Your head now dropped into the birth canal [diagram] and your mom could feel a lot of pressure down low.

Earlier we talked about the uterus as the place where you spent your first nine months before you were born. But the uterus wasn't just a safe place to be while you were growing from a zygote into a baby. It also had work to do. The uterus is really a muscle. In fact, it is the strongest muscle in your mother's body. The final signal for you to come out was given by the uterus, which started to contract—squeeze or get smaller. Each time the uterus contracted, it squeezed you and pushed you toward the opening of the birth canal.

This contracting or squeezing of the uterus is called "labor"... and it was a lot of hard work for your mom. As the uterus squeezed, your mom pushed to help you come out. Some women have very short labor but for others labor can last for hours—even all day and night. Be sure to ask your mom if you took a long time or came out quickly.

You may remember that you had been in the amniotic sac all these months and were surrounded by amniotic fluid. The uterus squeezed so strongly that the amniotic sac tore and allowed the fluid to run out. Your mom might explain that this was when her "water broke."

All that fluid in your lungs was squeezed out by the contractions of the uterus. In a little while your head could be seen coming out of the birth canal. A few more pushes and out you came! You probably took a deep breath... and cried! That's all right. We were glad you were here.

a closer look

Cesarean Section: Sometimes difficulties prevent babies from being born through the birth canal. These babies have to come out, so another way must be found. They are born by a surgery called "cesarean section" or "C-section". A small incision is made in the mother's abdomen and uterus, and within moments the baby is lifted out. The placenta is then removed, and the incisions are stitched back together.

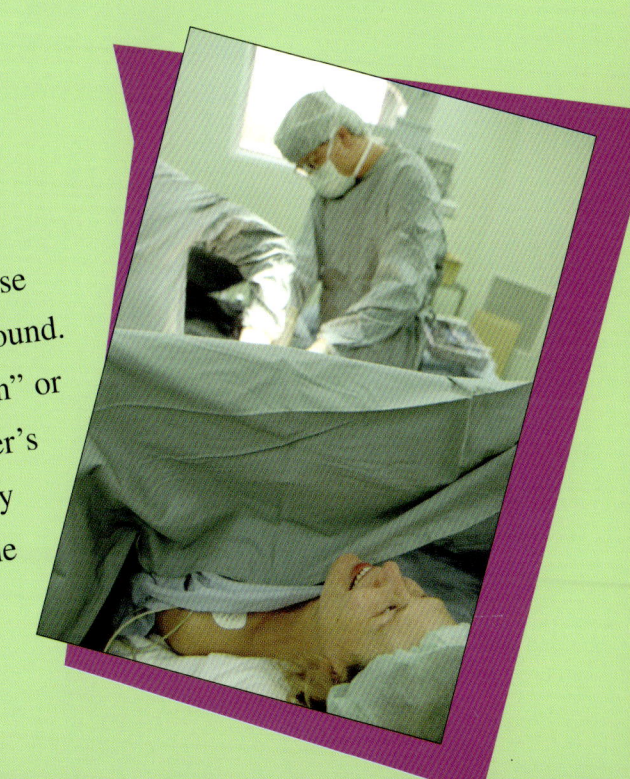

Adoption:
There are times when a mom and a dad, for various reasons, cannot have children through the process described in this book. So they may decide to adopt a baby. Other parents choose to make their family bigger by including children they did not conceive. These parents are blessed with children who come into their lives through adoption. Adoption is the process of becoming a parent of a child to whom someone else gave birth.

Your awesome, amazing life started long before you were born . . . long before your first birthday. You were an important person from the moment you were conceived . . . from the moment God handpicked you. God had a plan for you right from the start, a plan that is still unfolding today!

RACIAL DISCRIMINATION IN CANADA

ASIAN MINORITIES

Kananur V. Chandra, Ph.D.

1973

San Francisco

Printed in 1973 by

R AND E RESEARCH ASSOCIATES

4843 Mission St., San Francisco 94112

18581 McFarland Ave., Saratoga, CA 95070

Publishers and Distributors of Ethnic Studies

Editor: Adam S. Eterovich

Publisher: Robert D. Reed

Library of Congress Card Catalog Number

73-76006

ISBN

0-88247-208-9

Copyright 1973

Dedicated to the Peoples of the World

ACKNOWLEDGMENT

This study would not have been possible without the financial assistance of its sponsors, The Canada Council. The author extends his sincere appreciation for the genuine interest shown by the sponsors.

The author is also deeply grateful to East Indian, Pakistani and Bangla Desh immigrants who cooperated in the research study by giving their valuable time for interviews. Their helpfulness and friendly understanding helped to make this study possible.

Appreciation is extended to the employers, labor union officials, staff of Manpower and Immigration Centers, estate agents, employment agencies and officials of the housing offices who were kind enough to allow me to interview them.

The author is thankful to M/s. Research Associates, Inc., London, for permitting to use their PEP report Racial Discrimination in Britain.

Finally it is a pleasure to record my indebtedness to many individuals and friends who made this study possible by their generous help and cooperation.

Kananur V. Chandra

TABLE OF CONTENTS

Chapter		Page
I	INTRODUCTION	1
	Method of the Study	1
	Individual Questionnaire-Interviews with Colored Immigrants	3
	Personal Interviews With Potential Discriminators	4
	Field Tests	5
II	INTERVIEWS WITH COLORED IMMIGRANTS	7
III	EMPLOYMENT AND THE EXPERIENCES OF IMMIGRANTS	19
IV	GENERAL ATTITUDES AND PRACTICES IN THE EMPLOYMENT OF COLORED PEOPLE	37
V	LABOR UNIONS	45
VI	MANPOWER AND IMMIGRATION CENTERS	48
VII	HOUSING OF COLORED PEOPLE	51
	SUMMARY AND CONCLUSIONS	57
	APPENDIX	62

LIST OF TABLES

Tables		Page
1.	Life in Canada Compared With Expectations	9
2.	Sources of Disappointment with Life in Canada	11
3.	Reasons for Belief in Color Discrimination	13
4.	Changes in Ease of Life in Canada	17
5.	Reasons for a Belief That Life in Canada Has Become Easier	18
6.	Last Employment in Their Homeland Compared with Current Employment in Terms of Industry	21
7.	Classification of Immigrants' Jobs Before Immigrating to Canada	21
8.	Claims of Experience of Discrimination in Employment	23
9.	Percentage of Employers Who Might Discriminate Against Colored People in Giving Jobs	23
10.	Personal Experience of Discrimination in Employment Broken Down by Length of Time in Present Job	25
11.	Language Spoken and Claims of Personal Experiences of Discrimination	26
12.	Grounds for Claiming Refusal of Work	30
13.	Experiences in Employment Tests	33
14.	Personal Contacts With Landlords (40 contacts)	52
15.	Findings of Telephone Inquiries to Landlords	53
16.	Results of the Tests With Estate Agents	54
17.	Results of Tests With Housing Offices	54
18.	Claims of Discrimination in Housing	55

CHAPTER I

INTRODUCTION

During my stay in Canada, I had the opportunity to conduct several studies on foreign nationals, especially people from Asia and Africa. Many of them complained about discrimination in employment and aspects of social life in Canada. They attributed these misfortunes to their racial origin and skin color. These allegations of the colored immigrants led the researcher to conduct this study. According to Canadian laws, practice of discrimination in any form based on race, religion or national origin, is illegal and can be punished. But the practice of racial discrimination cannot be stopped by laws alone when it exists in the minds and actions of people. The aim of this study was to find out whether racial discrimination exists in Canada; if so, how extensive is it.

METHOD OF THE STUDY

The method used in conducting this study had three phases or approaches. In the first phase of the study, questionnaire-interviews were conducted among the colored immigrants (East Indians, Pakistanis and Bangladeshis) in the city of Montreal, Quebec, Canada. The purpose of the interviews was to find out the experiences of the immigrants who are the potential victims of any discrimination. This phase in itself would not prove, however, the existence of discrimination in Canada since the immigrant might exaggerate if things had not gone well for him or not be aware of much discrimination if he had stayed among his own people.

To remedy the inadequacy of the first phase of the study--talking to the colored immigrants about their life in Canada--the research team decided to gather the opinions of the white Canadians who are in a position to practice discrimination, namely, employers, labor unionists, landlords and others. This was done through personal interviews with them. Here, one should not expect to get a true picture of the situation but at least it presents their view of the problems they face in dealing with colored people. In this part of the study, valuable information about the attitudes and problems of the potential discriminators could be gathered.

The two parts of the study--personal interviews with colored immigrants and potential discriminators--would explain to the reader how the colored immigrants felt themselves affected by discrimination and how any discriminators justified their behavior. By looking at the surveys carefully the research team felt that the information gathered through the two surveys is valuable but it is doubtful that they provide us with accurate information on the extent of discrimination; in addition, the findings could be variously interpreted by those with different background or interests. To avoid this bias, the team had decided not to depend entirely on the findings of the personal interviews with the people but to put the matter to the test in a way that would provide objective evidence. One way of using the tests to find out whether discrimination occurred was to send people (both colored and white) of equal qualifications but different colors or national origin to apply for employment, housing and other services as the case might be and find out what happened to them. For example, if a colored person had applied for a job and the job had been refused but later the same job was offered to a white person with equal or fewer qualifications, then one could conclude that discrimination had occurred. Still it does not fully tell us whether the colored person had been refused a job because of his color or national origin. But, the two types of personal interviews with the people would throw some light on this aspect of the question. In the tests we had two testers; one was a white Canadian and the other a colored person.

The three surveys mentioned above constitute the method for this study on racial discrimination: Asian minorities. The three surveys are referred to as: Interviews with colored immigrants, Personal interviews with potential discriminators and the Field tests. The minority groups in the survey come from three Asian countries: India, Pakistan and Bangla Desh. A sample of 180 people was taken from a population of about 1800 East Indian, Pakistani and Bangledeshi people and each of them were interviewed in the appropriate language by people from their own countries. There were 76 interviews with potential discriminators in each of the fields of inquiry; experienced interviewers were used in the study. One hundred and forty field tests were carried out with our testers under close supervision.

There were no statistics available on the number of East Indian, Pakistani and Bangladeshi immigrants in the city. Therefore, we had to devise our own method to make a list of the above immigrants. First we made a list of the immigrants from the telephone directory. Each person in the list was contacted by telephone and asked several questions to ascertain his sex, age, origin of the country, current status in Canada (immigrant, non-immigrant or other), number of people in the household (adults and children), and the position held in Canada. Our interviewers also requested them to give the names and addresses of any friends or acquaintances from India, Pakistan and Bangla Desh residing in the city. In this way, we added many more people to our list as well as eliminated some from the list. Later, we contacted several organizations (consulates, ethnic clubs or associations, ethnic newspaper, friendship societies) to supply us with a list of the people from the countries surveyed. All of them were contacted by phone to determine their national origin, job, and other things mentioned above. In this way we were able to determine the approximate number of colored immigrants living in the city during the time of the survey, January, 1971 to January, 1972.

The colored immigrants from India, Pakistan and Bangla Desh live in all parts of the city. There are no ethnic enclaves or areas where a high proportion of immigrant population reside in the city. Therefore, the technique of random sampling was used in selecting the immigrants for personal questionnaire-interviews. The sample for the interviews come from different parts of the city. Consequently, no attempt had been made to divide the city into several areas and choose particular areas for the purposes of sampling.

A detailed description of the three surveys as well as the purposes and techniques of each survey are presented here.

INDIVIDUAL QUESTIONNAIRE-INTERVIEWS WITH COLORED IMMIGRANTS

The main aim of the personal interviews with colored immigrants was to find out the personal experiences of discrimination they had faced in Canada and to identify the types of people who suffered most severely. Apart from direct questioning on different aspects of discrimination, a number of general questions on reaction to life in Canada were included to ascertain how far discrimination was mentioned in their general comments on life in Canada.

It was found that one of the limitations of the interviews was that in many cases the discrimination was so subtle, the immigrants were not aware of the practices of discrimination. For instance if an employer says, 'no vacancy' or a landlord says 'the apartment or room is rented,' unless the immigrant has some way of knowing that the job is still open and the apartment is vacant, he has no way of knowing whether this is true or false. Our field tests concluded that open refusal on the grounds of race or color was very rare and in cases of higher positions it was virtually impossible to tell why the person was turned down even if he had better qualifications.

Immigrants who claimed personal experiences of discrimination were asked to give the evidence to support their claims. In this way, claims based on exaggeration or imagination were eliminated. A large number of claims were supported by strong evidence of discrimination. Many of the immigrants mentioned that their belief in discrimination was based on other people's experiences rather than their own.

A copy of the questionnaire is given in the appendix. Some of the topics covered in the questionnaire are: general questions on colored immigrant's experience of discrimination and personal information on the immigrants.

The questionnaire was constructed after personal interviews with a number of immigrants and one pilot questionnaire. After the preparation of the questionnaire, 180 colored immigrants were selected by using random sampling techniques.

PERSONAL INTERVIEWS WITH POTENTIAL DISCRIMINATORS

The personal interviews with people who are in a position to discriminate indicate the types of discrimination that take place and the justification or motive for such discrimination. These people are in a position to discriminate and also tell us authoritatively the discrimination practised by others in all areas.

The types of people who were interviewed include those in the following areas: (1) Employment - employers (both national and local); national and local labor unionists; the staffs of Manpower and Immigration offices and employment agencies, (2) Housing - landlords, estate agents and housing officers, and (3) Services - personnel in banks, insurance company officials.

People who were in a position to discriminate were personally interviewed by the testers to ascertain whether the colored immigrants present any problems to the employers and the action he takes to remedy the situation. The questions on the problems of colored immigrants were asked indirectly so that the employers did not know that the purpose of this survey was to investigate racial discrimination. The extent of discrimination disclosed by the employers should be taken as a bare minimum because they tend to minimize any discrimination practised.

Employers in the sample came from national as well as private sources. The labor unions were selected according to their coverage of occupations that immigrants tend to enter. The employment agencies and landlords were selected by using standard sampling techniques.

FIELD TESTS

The results of the field tests in this research study assume paramount importance due to their presentation of evidence as to the extent of discrimination. This information would supplement and support the findings of the other two phases of the survey, i.e., interviews with immigrants and the people who are in a position to discriminate. These tests are more scientific, in the sense that different variables in the study could be controlled under close supervision and the results could be verified. The variables were controlled by varying the occupational level and income of the colored testers and by including a white Canadian (both colored and white testers assume the same qualifications) in the tests to see whether color discrimination operates indiscriminately or whether it assumes a selective quality or is limited only to colored people.

The procedure used in the tests was to send both colored and white testers to apply for jobs and housing and, later, comparing their respective experiences to see whether there were any differences. In the tests both white and colored immigrants were matched according to the criterion of the job applications. Always, the colored tester applied first and the white Canadian tester second. Several steps were undertaken to keep the tests more relevant and scientific. Some of the steps were as follows:

1. Each tester reported directly his experiences without informing the second tester. In this way the bias due to expectations or assumptions by the second tester was eliminated.

2. If it was found that there was discrimination practiced then the discriminators, in many cases, were contacted to find whether they agreed that they had discriminated and, if so, what were the reasons for discrimination.

3. Both white and colored testers were chosen carefully paying attention to their age, appearance and competence in using the languages. In the tests, the testers were in the 28-32 age group, of similar heights and of good appearance. Both white Canadian and colored applicant spoke English and French languages but the colored immigrant had some accent.

In this study the field tests were very important in assessing the extent of discrimination though we were not able to find out the impact it has on the colored immigrant who suffered discrimination. In this way the three phases of the research study made it possible to find out whether discrimination exists in Canada, and what the extent of discrimination practised in several areas of life in the society is.

CHAPTER II

INTERVIEWS WITH COLORED IMMIGRANTS

When I was in India I was told that Canadians are kind, helpful and generous and treat all people equal. After my arrival in Canada I was disappointed to see the treatment we get from Canadians. We are discriminated in jobs, housing and other social aspects. They treat us like inferior beings from Asia.

This was a comment made by an immigrant to describe the color discrimination being practiced in Canada: a conviction which, the survey findings show, the large majority of the colored immigrants in Canada share. The term 'color discrimination' is used loosely by colored immigrants to describe a variety of situations they have faced in Canada such as discrimination in hiring and housing of colored people. They say that Canada is a country in which the white population, whether born Canadians or white immigrants, treat colored people with hostility and where those occupying positions of influence and authority discriminate against them. The kind of discrimination that worries them most is that encountered in obtaining and carrying out jobs and being accepted socially by the white Canadian society.

The hostility of the host community, discrimination in employment and the reluctance of Canadians to accept the colored people have convinced the large majority of the colored immigrants that color discrimination exists in Canada, and thus creates frustration and disillusionment among the colored immigrants in Canada. This is shown by the responses given to certain questions asked in interviews with a sample of immigrants. The questions asked were, "How does life in Canada compare with what you thought it would be like - is it better, about the same or worse than you expected?', and secondly 'Given your expectations as an arriving immigrant, what elements in Canadian life have come as a 'pleasant surprise' and thirdly, 'What elements in Canadian life have 'disappointed you.'

In the interviews with the immigrants, the researcher asked positive questions before he made any hints to discrimination or asked any detailed questions on specific areas of discrimination. The main purpose of the interviews was to get spontaneous and unprompted responses about the extent of discrimination the immigrants felt they experienced in Canada.

Further questions were asked to supplement the answers to the above questions at the end of the interviews. These were: 'In your view has it become easier or more difficult for a person from (name of the country) to live in Canada or hasn't it changed? What has made it like that?' and 'Would you say that there is any sort of color discrimination in Canada today? What makes you say that?'

The last question on 'color discrimination' prior to the classification data gives an opportunity to the people who were interviewed to talk about prejudice or discrimination uninhibited by the constraints of a formal, structured interview, while avoiding bias that such a question might have introduced into answers to subsequent questions, had it been asked at an earlier stage.

This chapter analyzes the responses of the colored immigrants to the general questions about prejudice and discrimination in Canadian society.

The responses show, in general terms, how far colored people are themselves concerned about discrimination in the fields which are the subject of the study in the survey. The findings of the interviews show that the problem of discrimination is one of immediate concern to them. The fact that a large proportion of colored minorities believe that Canada is not a just society would provide, in itself, a powerful argument for action being taken to ensure that justice is done, even if the beliefs were not fully justified.

The answers to the questions also provide an opportunity to describe the general attitudes and reactions of the East Indian, Pakistani and Bangladesh immigrants to life in Canada, and the differences between their respective expectations, aspirations and ways of life. The extent to which they want and expect to be treated as equals by Canadian people, and to participate in the Canadian way of life, influences the extent to which they find themselves in the type of situation where discrimination occurs.

Of all immigrants, under a third found their experiences below expectations, over a third found their experiences about the same as expected and a sixth had mixed feelings about their experiences. The following table gives the responses of the immigrants.

Table 1

Life in Canada Compared With Expectations

Expectations	Total No.:	East Indians 130 Per Cent	Pakistanis, Bangladeshis 50 Per Cent	
Better		4	1	5
About the same		33	9	42
Worse		24	7	31
Mixed feelings		13	2	15
No answer		6	1	7
			Total:	100

Note:
The figures appearing at the head of the table show the number of people on whom the expectations are based. The 'total number' refers to the actual number of people interviewed in each category.

For a question, 'Given your expectations as an arriving immigrant, what elements in Canadian life have come as a pleasant surprise,' a fifth of the immigrants said that no elements in Canadian life came as a pleasant surprise. For just over one-half of them economic and social aspects came as a pleasant surprise. They were very much impressed with the standard of living of the Canadian people and the freedom the Canadians have to do whatever they like and want.

The extent to which the colored people were unfavorably surprised seems to correlate closely with their expectations. A large number of immigrants had expected to be accepted, treated as equals, and, consequently to be able to participate fully in Canadian life. Because of their expectations, they made many attempts to participate in public life and social activities. This was particularly true of immigrants who came to Canada with university degrees. This group felt the impact of discrimination most strongly.

Most of the colored immigrants came to Canada to find employment and a good life which they felt was more difficult to obtain in their own countries. If they have found employment some of them did not even expect equal, fair or friendly treatment from Canadians but were resigned to the hostility and discrimination they experienced. Many respondents told the researcher that the question on discrimination was irrelevant because they came to Canada to find jobs. Others while wanting equal rights, were quite content with the company of their own countrymen in all aspects of Canadian life.

The study also shows, however, that the longer colored people lived in Canada the higher their expectations were and the more outgoing they became. This is shown by differences in the experiences of discrimination between relatively new immigrants and their counterparts. The new arrivals show a relatively low interest in the services available to them such as housing, and a consequent lack of awareness of discrimination. As their stay prolonged they become more interested in the services provided in the host community, and consequently the greater their awareness and experiences of discrimination.

In another question, "Given your expectations as an arriving immigrant, what elements in Canadian life have disappointed you," a large number of colored immigrants mentioned racial or cultural discrimination, and hostility or rejection because of race or color. The frequency with which racial or color prejudice and discrimination are mentioned by them is significantly high. Before considering the number of responses to the question, one should bear in mind that the question was asked before mention of prejudice or discrimination had been made and before the respondents were aware that experiences of discrimination represented any part of the interviews. The following table (page 11) demonstrates free and unprompted answers to the general questions.

The table (Table 2) indicates the extent of disappointment the colored immigrants have found with life in Canada. The most common sources of disappointment mentioned were color and racial prejudice in general, employment difficulties through prejudice or racial discrimination, and unfriendliness to foreigners.

In the sample 'color and racial prejudice' was the item mentioned most frequently after employment difficulties (35 per cent). The types of answers

Table 2

Sources of Disappointment with Life in Canada

Reasons	East Indians 130 %	Pakistanis Bangladeshis 50 %
Color and racial prejudice in general	43	45
Unfriendliness towards foreigners	24	20
Employment difficulties through prejudice or discrimination	35	25
Employment difficulties in general	14	9
Housing difficulties through prejudice or discrimination	12	10
Housing difficulties in general	12	6
Climate/food	2	1
General problems of adjustment	5	9
Social life disappointing	15	5
Religious difficulties (fanaticism of Canadians about their religion)	6	3

Note: Percentages add to more than 100 because some respondents mentioned more than one item.

assigned under the heading of 'color and racial prejudice' include references to 'the unfair treatment,' inequality in general,' and 'the way colored people can have only what white people don't want.' Unfriendliness of Canadians to foreigners came third (24 per cent) linked in many cases with prejudice or discrimination.

Many colored immigrants interviewed mentioned problems in getting jobs they are qualified for; a large majority of answers indicated that prejudice and discrimination due to race or color was the factor which prevented them from getting these jobs. They complain that they have to settle for those jobs, if they get any, which no white person wants or is available to take at that particular time. Those with higher occupational levels before coming to Canada were most concerned about preserving their own life style. Many times the immigrants did not spell out the source of difficulties to an interviewer who was also a colored person because they felt that the interviewer had certainly faced the same difficulties and thus it was unnecessary to elaborate. Therefore, there is a probability that many of the immigrants who referred to problems with jobs or rejection by Canadians were also reporting discrimination or prejudice, even if they did not specifically mention it.

The colored immigrants were also disillusioned with the hostility of other white immigrants towards them. It was painful for them to see that the white immigrants, especially English speaking or French, had better opportunities for advancement even though they lacked academic backgrounds equivalent to the colored immigrants.

A small number of the immigrants (eleven percent) said that nothing disappointed them in Canada. These were the people who came to Canada with lower expectations and ambitions and were satisfied with whatever they got in Canada. Some of the comments by these colored immigrants were:

> I came to Canada for employment. Now I work as a mechanic and I don't care if I am not treated equally by the whites here. I work and then go home. I have some friends from my own country and they are nice people. Other things like discrimination or prejudice don't matter to me.

> I don't have any university degree. Now I work as a laborer in a big store. I work overtime sometime. I make some money and take care of my family. I am not disappointed with some whites discriminating against me.

> Life is comparatively better here than in my country. I work, earn money and take care of my family. My children get good education here. I didn't come here to look for equality. As long as I have a steady job I don't care for anything else.

These comments by a small number of colored immigrants who experienced no disappointment to life in Canada can be explained by their limited ambitions and aspirations when they immigrated.

Table 3 (page 13) illustrates the reasons immigrants give for believing that color discrimination exists in Canada.

A number of colored immigrants think that many white Canadians are hostile and unfriendly towards them in all aspects of life; this hostility expresses

Table 3

Reasons for Belief in Color Discrimination

Reasons	East Indians %	Pakistanis Bangladeshis %
Discrimination in employment including recruitment, exploitation	69	20
Discrimination in housing	30	6
Discrimination in shops and public places	9	7
General hostility of host community:		
Prejudice, abuse, discrimination	39	41
General atmosphere in country unsympathetic to colored people	31	27
Aware of color prejudice and discrimination through mass media	9	7
Discrimination by officials (police, courts, public officials, etc.)	3	2
Discrimination in hotels, insurance, bank loans	8	3
Others: religious difficulties	6	3
Don't know	7	3

Note: Percentages add to more than 100 because some respondents mentioned more than one item.

itself in discrimination against them in everyday affairs, particularly in looking for employment or doing their work. Many of them agree that there are laws written into the books against racial or color discrimination but they do not deter the whites from discriminating against the colored population. According to the Canadian Bill of Rights, all the people are granted equal rights irrespective of color, creed, race or religion but in reality color discrimination does exist. Many of them felt that Canadians are hypocritical and dishonest in telling the world that racial discrimination exists in the United States but not on Canadian soil. They felt that open segregation is more honest than the hypocricy they alleged to be inherent in claiming to be a just, free society while practicing an informal and subtle color discrimination. This practice denied the colored immigrants equality of justice, education, jobs and a share in being a Canadian.

The percentages of the responses in Table 3 give reasons for the belief in color discrimination and the order of importance of the different aspects, on what had disappointed people on coming to Canada. Discrimination in employment is the largest single item mentioned by the people to represent the most widespread conviction that there is color discrimination in Canada. Colored immigrants feel that they face considerable hostility and discrimination in Canada because of their color and race.

Some whites do not agree with the charges of color discrimination or racial prejudice in Canada. They argue that the colored people coming to Canada from very different environments have big problems of adjustment and adaptation. Due to their inability to cope with the problems they face in Canada they use the claims of color discrimination or racial prejudice as an excuse. They rationalize their inadequacies and deficiencies by blaming other people and crying 'color discrimination' while in fact the discrimination and prejudice are illusory. The people who are in a position to discriminate level these charges against the colored immigrants and say that colored people carry 'chips on their shoulders' wherever they go.

But these charges by the white Canadians are not consistent with the findings of the second and third phases of our study. In the second phase many white Canadians themselves confessed that there is discrimination against colored people on a small scale by individuals who are in a position to discriminate even though there is legislation against discrimination. In the third phase of the survey--field tests --specific claims were checked by tests that were validated in 95 per cent of the cases. In other cases, the extent of color discrimination claimed by colored immigrants is shown to be substantially less than is indicated by the independent evidence. The experience of a white Canadian compared to the colored immigrant in the field tests demonstrates conclusively that the white Canadian experiences very much less discrimination than the colored person.

In the individual interviews with colored immigrants, many interesting responses were revealed by them about their experiences which were often humiliating and disgusting: from people speaking violence in classrooms, streets or at work to deprivation of basic necessities of existence, such as work and homes;

to abusing little colored children on their way home, the evidence of which is presented in subsequent chapters.

Some of the responses of the colored immigrants about their qualify of experiences are given here to illustrate the belief in color discrimination. Some of the personal abuses in everyday life made the greatest impact on them:

> My superior told me in front of everybody that if he becomes the Prime Minister of Canada, the first thing he would do is 'to ship all Indians and Pakistanis (includes Bangladeshis) back to their countries'.

> I earned a doctoral degree from a well-known North American university. I have extensive publications in Canada. Since I am a colored person some students would get up in the class and ask: "What degree do you have? You must be making lot of money here, etc." Some of these experiences are very humiliating. They would never dare to do this to a white professor even though he may be lousy. This happened to me in a prominent English university here.

> The Canadian mass media give a bad picture of our country and the people. When we go to shops or restaurants we can't ask for the things we are entitled to. They tell us, 'Do you have these things in your country?'. We pay for the things and would expect the same treatment usually they give to the whites.

> Even in courts of justice we don't get justice. If there is a case between a white and a colored person, the white man will get a better treatment from the court officials. They think that we are subhuman beings.

The most frustrating incidents were that some white people behaved friendly in certain circumstances but hostile in others:

> People tolerate us while we work with them. As soon as work is finished they try to avoid us in all walks of life.

> Sometimes neighbors look down upon us because they think we take away their jobs. They are jealous of colored immigrants.

> When I went to the Manpower Centre to look for job opportunities, the woman counselor told me 'Why don't you go back to your country? or go somewhere else'.

Some colored immigrants spent some time in the United States before coming to Canada as landed immigrants. Some of the comments of these immigrants were:

> In the United States, Negroes are considered as colored people. When I came to Canada I understood that if someone is not a white man then automatically he will be classified as a colored person. I feel that there is more subtle racism in Canada than in the United States.

A significant number of the immigrants were disappointed with discrimination in jobs. They felt the jobs available to them were: 'only the inferior,' the jobs which the whites did not want or the jobs which they could not get the white person to fill in. Also, they felt, they were the victims of 'last to be hired and first to be fired' attitude. Some of the comments are:

> I am working as a laborer for the last 2 years in a warehouse. I have a bachelor's degree from India and have taken many courses from Cornell through postal tuition. So far I could not get a suitable job for my education. Right here I have no prospect of promotion because I am the only colored man here. They don't want me here but I am here for a long time and belong to a labor union.

> Banks and big businesses do not hire us because they are very discriminative in their hiring practices. One personnel officer in a bank told me that I am under-qualified. After a month I went to the same bank for employment, the same person told me that I am over-qualified.

> When there was an acute shortage of teachers the school boards hired a number of colored people as teachers. Now they say our degrees are not recognized and they want to demote us. Eventually I am sure they replace all of us with white teachers from Britain, Australia, New Zealand, South Africa and the United States. This is how whites' democracy works for them!

According to the people who are in a position to discriminate, a large number of colored immigrants use the allegation of discrimination as an excuse for their inadequacies. This may be true with a small number of the colored people; perhaps the group with whom the white people came in contact were striving for total acceptance and leadership in the society. It could be that the whites allege the 'chip on the shoulder' to the colored as a pretext to practice discrimination and prejudice.

The answers to the questions on whether they thought life in Canada had become easier or more difficult for them, and what had caused the change, demonstrate the ways people actually cope up with discrimination and hostility. The following table would give the information.

Table 4

Changes in Ease of Life in Canada

Opinions	East Indians %	Pakistanis Bangladeshis %
Life easier	7	6
No change	16	1
Life more difficult	54	12
Uncertain	3	1
Total: 100 per cent	80	20

Only small number of people felt that life has become easier whereas a significant number of the colored people felt that life has become harder. These responses help us to assess the immigrants' evaluation of the direction of any change in their position and also show that time alone would not solve all the problems of the colored people.

The explanations given by the people who say that life has become easier are more important to study. These people who felt that life has improved could be divided into two groups. The first group did not give the reasons for improvement in their lives whereas the second group gives explanations for improvement; for instance, 'I earn more money and I work less,' 'now I have many friends from my own country.'

Wherever a reason is given for an improvement, the reason is the growth of their numbers which protects them from discrimination by associating with their own groups. Many of the colored immigrants look for jobs where they know other colored people work; they avoid situations in which they might confront discrimination. People who did not experience discrimination personally but were aware of it made such statements as:

I got the job through a friend. Now I go to work in the morning and spend the evenings at home or with my friends from my own country. I go where I am accepted and treated with respect. Color discrimination is much more subtle in Canada than in the United States.

Table 5

Reasons for a Belief That Life in Canada Has Become Easier

Reasons	East Indians	Pakistanis Bangladeshis
Total No.:	12	14
	%	%
Life easier because of easy job	34	40
Living standards have risen	32	20
Easy to get better education	29	32
People have become friendlier	13	15
Don't know	5	8
	113	115

Note: Percentages add to more than 100 because some respondents mentioned more than one item.

Although the colored people try to avoid exposure to discrimination in some aspects of life, they cannot avoid some contact with white Canadians in the community, at work or at public places. Exposure to these situations of potential discrimination make them believe in color discrimination or racial hostility in Canada.

CHAPTER III

EMPLOYMENT AND THE EXPERIENCES OF IMMIGRANTS

In the previous chapter the answers to the questions were general ones expressed in general terms. They show how far discrimination in employment features in people's general criticisms of life in Canada and give rise to a belief in color discrimination. But they do not explain what proportion of colored people are aware that they have personally suffered acts of discrimination.

Replies to more detailed, specific questions on employment and on the immigrants' experiences of discrimination in jobs will be discussed here. The data on discrimination presented here will be supplemented later by Manpower and Immigration officials, employment agencies, labor unions, and the employees themselves.

The answers of the immigrants in the interviews bring out two kinds of information pertinent to their experiences of discrimination in employment. The first describes the jobs they are doing in Canada now, as compared to the jobs they did before coming to Canada as landed immigrants. The second part of the information claims personal acts of discrimination against them. The questions in the interviews were concerned with hiring practices, promotion, type of work, and rate of pay. In addition, the claims of the immigrants will be assessed through the use of field tests to see whether employers or firms which refused colored people jobs in reality had a position available for which the immigrant was qualified.

The interviews were carried out in January-August, 1971; during that time 78 per cent of the colored immigrants were in regular employment. Consequently, 22 per cent of them were unemployed compared to the national figures of six to seven per cent during that same period. The unemployment percentage was over three times as high for these immigrants as for the nation as a whole.

	Per Cent
East Indians	80.00
Pakistanis & Bangladeshis	16.00
Total:	96.00

Moving to Canada has brought deterioration in living standards and an increase in unemployment: in the three months before coming to Canada, 96 per cent of the colored immigrants had regular employment. This deterioration of living standard is particularly evident for those at the upper level of skills. Immigrants with few or no skills were more apt to gain employment than those with technical or professional training.

The jobs the immigrants are doing in Canada are often different than the jobs they were doing and had trained for. Before emigrating to Canada, the immigrants were engaged over a wide range of industries, the seven most important being manufacturing, agriculture, technical, construction, service industries, government services and professional jobs. These industries accounted for 100 per cent of the previously employed immigrants. Now, professional areas and service industries dominate their jobs in Canada. The following table illustrates the seven most common industries before coming to Canada and after obtaining employment in Canada. It also shows the extent of change in industry after emigrating to this country. (See Table 6, page 21.)

A large number of immigrants are now in service industries and professional areas, such as engineering and teaching. All those who were in agriculture and government services before emigrating have now moved to other industries. These people have joined the manufacturing or service industries as unskilled or semi-skilled workers.

Even though a high percentage of persons remained in similar industries after immigration, many received cuts in both pay and status in Canada. For example, a professional who was a lecturer in an Indian university could not find that position in a Canadian university. He would often take courses in Canada leading to teacher certification and gain employment teaching in an elementary school. Similarly, an immigrant possessing an M.B.A. degree who had held a

Table 6

Last Employment in Their Homeland Compared with Current
Employment in Terms of Industry

Industry	Total No. of respondents:	Employment in Canada: 140 %	Employment in Home Country: 177 %
Agriculture		0	2
Government Service		0	5
Construction		10	11
Technical areas		11	8
Manufacturing		13	8
Service industries		27	22
Professional areas		39	44
Total		100	100

supervisory position in this country, might find work as a clerk in a manufacturing plant. In both these representative cases, the individual would be classified as working in the same industry even though his position and salary in that industry is lower.

In the personal interviews, the immigrants' jobs were classified as unskilled manual, skilled manual, and non-manual. The following table shows the classification of the immigrants' jobs before immigrating.

Table 7

Classification of Immigrants' Jobs Before
Immigrating to Canada

	Per Cent
Unskilled Manual	2
Skilled Manual	12
Non-manual	84
Other	2
Total	100

Many of the people who formerly held white collar positions are now employed as laborers or as unskilled manual workers in manufacturing, construction, or service industries.

Many of the colored people were forced to take manual jobs so that they could take care of themselves and their families. Not only has this situation created frustration and worries among them, but it is also a waste of human resources and training. Many of them were fully qualified and able to enter professional, administrative, or clerical work but they were unable to find employment in those areas. The interviews with people in Manpower Centers and employment agencies confirm the difficulties and the extent of discrimination faced by these people in seeking non-manual jobs.

Some of the findings are interesting to note. Nearly half of the colored people claimed they had personal experience of discrimination. They supported their claims by convincing evidence which was almost always confirmed in the field tests. The most able and best qualified people had the experience of discrimination on a wider scale.

In the personal interviews, questions were directed to find out whether employment was refused because of race or color. The questions asked to elicit this information were as follows:

1. The immigrants were asked whether they believed that there are any employers in Canada who would refuse a person a job just because of his race or color, rather than for some other reason.

2. If they answered 'yes', they were asked out of every hundred employers in Canada, how many they would guess discriminate against commonwealth immigrants seeking employment.

3. They were asked whether they know this from their own personal experience or from other people's experience.

4. If they claimed that their views on discrimination were based on personal experience, they were asked to give details of the 'personal experience'. If they answered that their views were based on other people's experience only, they were asked as to the reason why people they know have experienced discrimination in seeking employment, but they have not.

The responses to these questions are given in the following tables:

Table 8

Claims of Experience of Discrimination
in Employment

Total number of Respondents: 180	Per Cent
1. Personal experiences of discrimination claimed and evidence provided	41
2. Have only applied for jobs where it was known discrimination did not occur	4
3. Avoided discrimination	12
4. Belief in discrimination through the knowledge of the experiences of others only	25
5. Uncertain about the existence of discrimination	9
6. No belief in discrimination	9
Total	100

A question was asked to guess the percentage of employers who discriminate against colored immigrants in Canada. The answers are as follows:

Table 9

Percentage of Employers Who Might Discriminate
Against Colored People in Giving Jobs

Total number of respondents:	East Indian 114 %	Pakistani Bangladeshi 37 %
95 per cent or more	6	2
85-94 per cent	12	0
45-84 per cent	28	6
20-44 per cent	14	5
1-19 per cent	20	1
None	2	4
Total	82	18

The purpose of several questions asked in the questionnaire was to find out first what proportion of people had experienced acts of discrimination that they could substantiate and secondly how those who were aware of discrimination avoided it. The personal interviews with the immigrants were conducted in such a fashion that the immigrants were neither led nor offended by the questions.

The answers to the questions revealed that forty-one per cent of the colored immigrants had undergone personal experience of discrimination and provided evidence to support their claims. Another sixteen per cent avoided discrimination by seeking employment at places where many of their countrymen were already working.

A fairly large proportion of people in the sample were uncertain whether discrimination existed or they thought it did not exist - eighteen per cent of the respondents felt this way (see table 9 for percentages). The reason for the lack of knowledge of discrimination was that they secured employment through the help of their friends or lived among their own people and thus did not come into contact with discrimination in employment or housing. This explanation is supported by the answers to similar questions on private rental of housing. A large percentage of those who were uncertain about discrimination by landlords, or who did not think it occurred, had never applied for accommodation to a white landlord who was a stranger.

Local variations in the incidences of discrimination in housing were found in the study. In certain areas of the city the experience of discrimination was higher than in others. Similarly, certain types of jobs were denied to the colored immigrants because employers were able to find white people to occupy the positions. Those jobs which were demanding and done under the worst physical surroundings to such an extent that they were almost unacceptable to white people were given to the colored immigrants. Sometimes certain better jobs were given to the immigrants because the employers were not able to find qualified whites to fill the jobs. In such cases, immigrants were not sure whether an employer would refuse someone a job purely on the basis of race or color.

Those immigrants who have been in Canada for a longer time and who tried to move outside the role that is prescribed for them, by aspiring to get better jobs, have exposed themselves much more frequently to the possibility of discrimination.

There is a relationship between claims of discrimination and the length of time immigrants had been working on their present jobs. People who stayed in their jobs for more than seven months and up to three years and those who sought work recently were more likely to claim experiences of discrimination. The actual percentages are given in the following table.

Table 10

Personal Experience of Discrimination in Employment
Broken Down by Length of Time in Present Job

Length of time in present job	Proportion Per Cent
6 months or less	9
7-12 months	12
Over 1 year - up to 3 years	19
Over 3 years	7
Total	47

Note: Totals do not add up to 100 per cent because only personal experience of discrimination is added.

A large number of immigrants have stayed in their jobs for between one and three years. This picture contrasts sharply with the image employers hold of immigrants. Many employers in the interviews said that colored immigrants were inefficient, unreliable, docile, dependent and temperamentally incapable of concentrating on anything. The information in the preceding table does not support this stereotype.

It is important to note that the proportion of people who claimed experience of severe discrimination are those people who are the ablest. A significant number of employers reported that the three main difficulties involved in employing East Indian, Pakistani and Bangladesh immigrants were their lack of English and/or French language proficiency, their lack of qualifications (Canadian educational institutions do not recognize East Indian, Pakistani and Bangladesh university degrees) and their lack of Canadian experience (whatever it means) before coming to Canada. Employers argue that these were the reasons why they had to refuse the colored immigrants and that it was not color or racial origin. It is important to note that those immigrants who earned their degrees in Canadian universities and improved their English and/or French speaking abilities, had experienced more discrimination.

The survey shows that the claims of discrimination were least among those immigrants whose first language was a native one and most common among those whose first language was English. The following table shows the proportion claiming personal experience of discrimination.

Table 11

Language Spoken and Claims of Personal Experiences of Discrimination

Language spoken as a child	Proportion claiming personal experiences of discrimination Per Cent
Native language spoken both at home and at school	40
Native language spoken at home; English first language at school	50
English spoken at home and at school	80

Thus, those people with the highest educational qualifications, and in particular those with English, university and professional qualifications, encountered personal experience of discrimination.

An analysis of the educational qualifications of the people and their claims of discrimination reveal the following:

1. The lowest proportion of people with secondary school qualifications made claims of personal experience of discrimination; 22 per cent.

2. The group in which the next highest proportion made claims were those with:

     a. professional qualifications from their country or origin: 35 per cent.
     b. other vocational training: 31 per cent.

3. The groups in which the highest proportion made claims were those with:

     a. American or Canadian trade qualifications: 75 per cent.
     b. Degree from the United States and Canada: 78 per cent.
     c. Degrees from country of origin: 85 per cent.

Among the six groups with the highest proportion of claims of discrimination, however, are people with university degrees and technical qualifications obtained in their countries of origin before emigrating to Canada. It poses a real problem when it comes to comparing the qualifications between different countries, especially between developing and industrially advanced countries. So far there are no international standards available to determine the equivalency of educational qualifications throughout the world accurately. The lack of these educational standards in assessing the educational qualifications from other developing countries can be used as a weapon by employers, labor unions and others to discriminate against the colored immigrants and claim with perfect justice that they were not discriminating but only applying agreed principles to people with differing qualifications.

People with indigenous qualifications always looked more widely for jobs and in most cases ended up applying for jobs below the levels of their qualifications. They claim to have experienced discrimination on a larger scale and they were also more sensitive to experiences of discrimination.

Those people who earned their degrees either from the United States or Canada were much more likely to have sought jobs at least at their level of qualifications. The employers interviewed in the survey responded that when immigrants earn their qualifications from North American institutions they would have no difficulty in obtaining jobs in Canada, yet a large majority of those people who obtained their degrees in North American institutions said that they have been refused jobs because of race or color of the skin.

1. <u>East Indian</u>, Aged 25, Came to Canada in 1968, Holds a Master's Degree From a Canadian University in Geophysics

    Applied to a big company for a job in his area of studies. He was called by the personnel officer. The officer said, "We take only Canadians." The East Indian replied, "I am a landed immigrant here." The officer said, "Still you are not a Canadian."

    The East Indian is now working as a salesman in a clothing store.

    The same company was approached by the testers in the follow-up testing. The white Canadian was told that jobs were available if he would like to apply. The colored person was told that there were no jobs available.

2. <u>East Indian</u>, Aged 30, Came to Canada in 1969; Holds a Diploma in Auto Mechanics

    Applied for a job in an automobile plant: "I was told that preference would be given to people who spoke French and English fluently. I told them that I am fluent in English. They said that I should be fluent in French."

3. <u>Pakistani</u>, Aged 25, Came to Canada in 1970; Holds a Master's Degree in Commerce From a Reputable English University

    He called a private organization on the phone for a position. He was told: "We do not employ East Indians, Pakistanis or Bangladeshis."

    Now the informant is employed in the type of work for which he had originally applied. The organization in question was called on the phone by our testers in a follow-up test. The English Canadian was told that jobs were available if he wished to apply. The Pakistani tester was told that there were no openings in the type of work he was seeking (the same as that of the English Canadian) at that organization.

4. <u>Man From Bangla Desh</u>, Aged 27, Came to Canada in 1968; Holds a University Degree in Mechanical Engineering

    He applied to a big factory as a draftsman where he was told: "We give preference to our people (white first). Sorry we can't offer you a job at this time."

5. <u>East Indian</u>, Aged 38, Came to Canada in 1970; He Obtained His Degree in Teaching From Britain

He applied for a teaching position with a school board. He was told: "Our policy is to give jobs to Canadian trained teachers only."

The person is now working as a teacher with a different school board. It was confirmed by the researcher that another Englishman with the same qualifications was offered a teaching position by the first school board.

6. <u>East Indian,</u> Aged 27, Came to Canada in 1964; Holds a Master's Degree in Business Administration From a Candian University

He applied for a job with a company and was told: "You should have a knowledge of the French language." When he told them that he is fluent in French, he was again told, "You do not have Canadian Experience."

While looking at the immigrants' experience of discrimination, the researcher has presented the data in terms of "claims of discrimination". Many of these claims are validated by evidence produced by the immigrants themselves and by the results of the field tests which were carried out to see what would happen when people of different colors and nationalities applied for jobs from the employers against whom claims had been made.

Those immigrants who had claimed to have had personal experience of discrimination were asked to give details of their experience, including the name of the firm, type of firm, the method of application, the type of work applied for, the person seen by the informant and the evidence for the claim of discrimination. A breakdown of the answers given in response to questions is supplied in the appendix.

The analysis of the answers for the questions asked reveals that only 42 per cent of the firms were named by the immigrants. A large majority of the immigrants did not wish to give the names of the firms involved because of the fear of repraisals either by the government or the employers. Secondly, the majority of the applications were made for the kind of job in the section of industry where all our evidence has shown immigrants to be the most acceptable: engineering and professional jobs in industry and educational institutions. Thirdly, the people who discriminated against the immigrants came from all levels of the work force: directors, managers, board members, deans, heads of departments, professors, receptionists, clerks or secretaries and people in personnel offices.

It is significant to note the answers people gave to justify their claims that they had been refused jobs because of their race or color. The most common answers that they had been told were: 'No Indians, Pakistanis or (Bangladeshis)', 'unsuitable' (without being asked for any details of skills, qualifications or experience), 'no Canadian experience' and 'no vacancies' (when the immigrants knew there were openings). The responses of the employers provide strong evidence to warrant the immigrants having drawn the conclusions that they did. The different grounds claiming discrimination and the proportion falling into each category are as follows:

Table 12

Grounds for Claiming Refusal of Work

Claims	Per Cent
1. Was told 'no colored'	3
2. Was told 'no East Indians or Pakistanis (and Bangladeshis)	12
3. Was offered the job over the phone or in writing but turned down when seen to be colored	8
4. Was told 'unsuitable' without being asked for any details of skills, qualifications, or experience	12
5. Was told 'have many colored already'	5
6. Was told 'no vacancies' when he knew there were vacancies because:	
a. continued to be advertised	7
b. someone he knew got the job after him	7
c. someone he knew at the firm told him	5
d. white men applying with him got the jobs	10
7. Was told "We'll let you know"/"We'll send for you" and never heard from them	8
8. Should be fluent in "French"	5
9. No Canadian experience	10
10. Need only 'Canadian citizens'	8
Total	100

The above table is self-explanatory but still it is necessary to interpret the answers in certain categories. First is the group of answers that depend on knowledge that a position existed because a job continued to be advertised after they were told none was available. Among these people there could have been some who had replied to a newspaper advertisement with an established advance booking whether the jobs had been filled or not; thus an employer might book an advertisement every day for a wekk in a newspaper and even if all positions were filled by mid-week it would still be run for the rest of the week. However, although the immigrants did not always mention the type of advertisement they had seen, it appeared to be normally the "notice boards outside the factory gate" type rather than a newspaper advertisement.

Secondly, where it was claimed that white applicants were offered jobs whereas the non-white applicants were not, it is quite possible that the white applicants were justifiably preferred to the non-white applicants. The actual claims, however, show that the informants were using the fact that white applicants secured employment merely as evidence that jobs were available when they had been told that none were available. This, like other categories, is illustrated in the following cases:

1. Sent by the Manpower Center for a job as a laborer in a factory. When they saw I was an East Indian they said: "Sorry, we already have many colored people here." The man at the Manpower Center said he was sure that the job was still open.

2. Applied to a large hotel for a job as porter. The head porter at that time told me that there were no jobs available. That same day I applied again but to a different head porter and was given the job. I was told by another porter that there was a job available the first time.

3. I applied to a bank (with a university degree in commerce received in Pakistan and enough credits to receive a degree at McGill University) for clerical work or any other work. I was told that I was under-qualified. I went to the same place a month later and I was told that I was over-qualified.

4. I applied for a teaching position in a university. (I earned a Ph.D. in the United States). I was told by the chairman of the department, "East Indians have language problem, therefore we do not like to hire them." I speak good English and I have spent three years teaching at a well-known American university.

5. An applicant went to a private employment agency to apply for any kind of work. "There were fifteen of us and there were three colored including myself. Four of the whites came after us. The man-in-charge called us and told us to wait in the corner. Then he sent all the whites to job vacancies and then called us and told us that there were no job openings."

6. I went to a big automobile corporation to apply for a job as salesman and I was stopped by the French receptionist who said, "It is no use going in there because there is no employment office here. Even if there was one, they wouldn't hire you because you don't speak French." At that time another white man came for a job. The receptionist told him to go in for a job interview.

7. I saw advertisement in a newspaper for a chemist and I wrote to the company for the job. I received a letter acknowledging my inquiry saying that there was a position open and that I should contact them by phone. On the phone I was asked if I was a Canadian. When I said that I was a landed immigrant from Bangla Desh, I was told, "Sorry, we don't hire foreigners."

8. I went to a food chain company to apply for laborer's work. There was a white man there as well. I was told 'no jobs available'. Then I waited for the white man and he told me he got a laborer's job.

The above are the answers immigrants gave to justify their claims that they had indeed undergone discrimination. The claims of the immigrants and the field tests conducted by the testers provide a strong prima facie case that discrimination did occur and that a large proportion of the claims are valid.

Field tests were conducted to investigate the claims of discrimination. We selected a sample of the firms mentioned in the claims and sent two testers to each one to inquire about jobs or apply for jobs. One tester was a white Canadian fluent in the French as well as in the English languages, the second was an East Indian or Pakistani or Bangladeshi of the same level of competency as the white Canadian.

The outcome of the field tests showed that in six out of every ten cases follow up, the claims of the immigrants (that they had been refused jobs because of race or color) were justified. The responses which each tester received from each firm or organization were classified in one of three ways:

    a. He was offered a job or told to apply for a vacancy.

b. He was told there was no vacancy immediately available but was advised to fill out an application form or was told there were no vacancies for non-Canadians.

c. He was told there was no vacancy.

Table 13 shows the number of occasions on which each of the two types of testers experienced each of these three responses.

Table 13

Experiences in Employment Tests

Response	White Canadian	East Indian, Pakistani or Bangladeshi
	Number of occasions each response experienced	
A. Offered a job or told to apply for a vacancy	13	2
B. Told 'No vacancy at present' but advised to fill out an application form or Told 'No vacancy for non-Canadians'	5	6
C. Told 'No Vacancy'	6	16

Only in two out of twenty-four firms tested was the colored immigrant tester told that a vacancy existed and was offered a job. The white Canadian tester received thirteen offers. On six occasions the colored immigrant was told that there was no vacancy immediately available but was advised to fill out an application form or he was told that there were no vacancies for non-Canadians. This latter incident occurred only _five_ times for the Canadian tester. On six occasions there was no vacancy for anyone. Thus the incidence of discrimination on the part of these firms was as follows:

Number of cases where no job was available for anyone	6
Number of cases where employment was possible	18
Discrimination against the white Canadian tester	1
Discrimination against the colored tester	9

Please note that the firms tested included some that were interviewed in the survey of potential discriminators: employers who both employed some colored immigrants and stated categorically that they did not discriminate. Yet in the field tests East Indian, Pakistani or Bangladeshi applicants suffered discrimination from these same employers. The conclusion that emerges from the tests is that just because a firm employs colored people in some capacity does not mean that it does not discriminate against colored people for certain types of jobs or at certain points in time. It also proves that either superior administrative officials in these firms were unaware of practices adopted by individuals at varying levels of authority in their organizations or that they were misleading the interviewers.

Number of occasions job offered:

        White Canadian   13
        Colored immigrant 2

A small number of colored immigrants felt that they have not been discriminated against because they had qualities which made them superior to their countrymen. These immigrants felt that being discriminated against is held to be a sign of low status or inferiority and that an admission to having suffered discrimination involves a loss of self-esteem or a loss of face. This feeling was expressed in the reports of interviewers who conducted the survey.

The findings of the field tests along with the claimants' evidence show that a significant majority of the claims of discrimination were justified. Other findings point to the conclusion that the proportion of immigrants who claimed personal experience of discrimination understate the extent of the problem, for three reasons:

1. <u>Lack of Knowledge</u>:
    Unless the refusal of work is accompanied by a direct statement of discrimination, the colored immigrant does not know that he is being discriminated against. In the field tests where the testers applied for jobs, the colored testers did not know that they had been discriminated against until each tester's independent findings were subsequently analyzed. This demonstrates that it is difficult for an immigrant to know that he is being discriminated against when he is applying for a position.

2. <u>Avoidance of Discrimination and Lack of Exposure to the Open Job Market</u>:

    A small number of colored immigrants had come to Canada with pre-arranged jobs. Therefore, they had never been in a position where they could have been discriminated against. Those people who were not aware of discrimination even through the experience of others, intentionally avoided discrimination by applying for work only where they were sure that they would have no problem in getting jobs. This shows that some immigrants had regulated their lives in order to avoid discrimination and thus did not expose themselves to the open job market.

3. <u>Types of Jobs</u>:

A large number of immigrants had been looking for professional jobs in industry and in educational institutions and it was here that they had experienced substantial discrimination. Only a small number of the respondents were seeking partly skilled jobs in various places, but they also met with discrimination while seeking jobs.

After an analysis of discrimination in employment it was discovered that the people with the greatest ability were the ones who experienced discrimination the most. Experience of discrimination was most frequent among people with the highest educational qualifications and less frequent among those with no formal qualifications.

In terms of English speaking ability, experience of discrimination was most common among people who were fluent in speaking and understanding the English language.

It was found that the longer the time spent in Canada, the more discrimination they faced.

A significant number of responses from employers indicated reasons other than discrimination as justification for refusing jobs to colored immigrants. They stated that the lack of qualifications, English and French speaking ability and knowledge of western ways of life were the main reasons for not giving employment to East Indian, Pakistani and Bangladesh peoples. They also stated that the immigrants' "chip-on-the-shoulder" attitude would not change and that the immigrants' claim that they experience discrimination when they had been refused jobs even when the refusal was made for perfectly valid reasons.

The reactions of the employers were in sharp contrast with the findings of the field tests; and there is no evidence in the findings that the immigrants were over-eager to attribute their hardships to color and to make invalid claims of discrimination. Along with the results supplied before, their responses to the questions on beliefs in discrimination and in the extent of discrimination were related to their personal experiences or to knowledge of other people's experiences.

In conclusion, a large number of colored immigrants claimed experience of discrimination and their claims are mostly justified. Those people who have higher academic qualifications and speak English fluently are the ones who experience discrimination the most.

CHAPTER IV

GENERAL ATTITUDES AND PRACTICES IN THE EMPLOYMENT OF COLORED PEOPLE

Many of the colored immigrants who were interviewed had been very disappointed about their experience of life in Canada and of the white people with whom they had come into contact. The results of the field tests showed that a large number of immigrants were justified in their complaints that they had been discriminated against when applying for jobs.

This research study would have been incomplete without the employers' view of the situation, together with that of other Canadians who deal with problems relating to the employment of immigrants. Therefore, we interviewed a significant sample of employers, labor unionists, Manpower and Immigration officials and representatives of employment agencies.

Our research team interviewed 51 employers, 10 labor unionists (national as well as local level), staff in 10 employment agencies and counselors in five Manpower and Immigration Centers. The purpose of these interviews was: to find out the policies and practices of the employers toward the employment of colored immigrants, and in particular how far they might practice discrimination; to discover how people in each category viewed the policies and practices of people in other categories; and, to elicit any justifications that people had for their discriminatory practices.

A large number of the informants said that they believe that all people should be treated equally and that the Constitution of Canada guarantees equal rights to all the people in the country. Most people in the personnel offices knew that an infringement of such a law would complicate their jobs and a survey on the extent of discrimination might damage the name of their organizations.

Due to the reasons mentioned, the employers were reluctant to make direct statements that they themselves discriminated. Some employers were frank enough to comment on discrimination against the colored immigrants by other people. A small number of officials--labor unionists, staff of employment agencies and Manpower and Immigration officials--did admit that there is discrimination against colored people on a very small scale. They also said that they are not in a position to take action against those employers who discriminate against colored immigrants because the employers do not directly tell them that they do not employ colored people. Therefore, it made it difficult for the Manpower and Immigration officials to take action against the employers. It is reasonable to believe that no employer would willingly admit that he had discriminated against the colored people.

In view of these influences on the employers, it seemed unlikely that we could find out such things as the percentage of firms that discriminate in employment by asking questions from a structured questionnaire. Therefore, our approach took the form of informal discussions centered on the problems which immigrants presented to the respective employers in their jobs, and the policies and practices that they adopted to deal with these problems.

Experienced interviews were used to conduct the informal interviews with officials who were in a position to discriminate against the immigrants in employment. These interviews produced direct statements of different forms of discrimination and a particular policy of discrimination adopted by the employers, but these responses must be taken to be minimal. The practices are certainly more widespread than these minimal responses suggest. Moreover there is the evidence of the field tests, which contradicted the statements of some of the employers.

In the interviews the employers were at ease to talk about the problems that immigrants presented. A large number of employers and Manpower staff members agreed in their assessment of the characteristics of immigrants. The general characteristics attributed to the immigrants by these informants is discussed in this chapter.

The general characteristics were of two main types: occupational and personal. By occupational characteristics are meant qualities which are relevant to the effectiveness of immigrants in the jobs they hold or try to obtain. By personal characteristics are meant personality, character or physical qualities which are attributed to immigrants and which make them attractive or unattractive to the informant as people. The personal characteristics can of course become occupational characteristics in jobs where ability to get along with people is important.

The occupational characteristics generally attributed to immigrants were: a lack of understanding of the Canadian way of life and in particular poor spoken English and lack of French speaking ability, low standard of their indigenous degrees, a tendency to over-claim qualifications, and high occupational mobility. Other characteristics included slowness, carelessness, withdrawal tendencies, lack of initiative, and more interest in theoretical type of work than practical work. The personal characteristics generally included strange food habits which manifested itself in weakness of physical stamina, dirtiness, inferiority complex, or a marked sensitivity to color which made them attribute all failures or misfortunes to that.

Often the informant would deny that he held the stereotyped views of immigrants but was handicapped in hiring or placing the immigrant because of the prejudice of others. For example, an employer would say that, whatever his views, other people--his other white employees, his friends, his clients--believed in the stereotype of immigrants, making them undesirable. Whether this tendency of the informants to project the objectional characteristics of the immigrants to other people was based on fear, assumption, or experience, it gave rise to what emerged as perhaps the most consistent justification for discrimination: hostility or resistance by the white people towards the colored immigrants. It is important and useful to discuss further the characteristics attributed to colored immigrants.

A significant number of informants mentioned language as the greatest single difficulty connected with the employment of immigrants from these countries. Local employers stated that although fluent English or French was not always essential in manual or semi-skilled work, the poor language skills of most immigrants impeded promotion and often made it necessary to use another member of the staff. Evidence gathered during the field tests, however, contradicted the statements of some of the informants.

Some officials of the employment agencies and Manpower and Immigration Centers also said that because of lack of fluency in the English or French languages, most immigrants seeking employment were, inevitably, rejected to compelled to accept employment at lower levels than their academic qualifications. This was one of the main complaints against the colored people being considering for employment.

The second difficulty, again mentioned by all groups of informants was that a high proportion of those colored immigrants seeking employment were not qualified for the jobs applied for. They said that the degrees earned from their home countries were not recognized in Canada and they fell short of the requirements demanded for employment in Canada. This lack of qualifications and disparity of training standards between Canada and developing countries often made it necessary to employ the immigrant at a level below that at which he felt he was qualified, or not employ him at all. This point was made with regard to both skilled technicians and professionally qualified people.

The third difficulty mentioned in employing the immigrants was "lack of Canadian experience." This difficulty is closely related to the qualification and disparity of training standards between Canada and the native countries of the colored immigrants. In the personal interviews with the employers, no clear cut definition of "Canadian experience" was given by any group of informants. Some employers said that the immigrants lack a knowledge of Canadian customs, culture or standards. All of them agree that the immigrants must have "Canadian experience" but they were not ready to provide an opportunity to the immigrants to acquire this "Canadian experience".

There is a close relation between occupational characteristics and personal qualities. The following quotations from the employers illustrate the point:

"They are lazy and do not take their jobs seriously."

"They are very shy and do not mix with other workers. They are interested only in making money. They do not participate in any of the company's activities."

"They want only clerical jobs. They do not like to work with their hands."

"Sometimes we have to spend a long time in explaining things to them. They do not understand either the language or work standards. You have to tell them everything four or five times."

"They are after money. They move from one place to another all the time. They do not stay in one place for long. How can you hire them?"

"Some of the employees complain about smell. It may be what they eat that makes them smell. It is a very delicate matter. In such cases I usually made it a point to tell them indirectly."

"Some immigrants from India come for jobs with turbans and beards too. They do not want to change their ways. Many of our employees object to their appearance. They say they smell."

"They always want a big job. They say they have university degrees. If we say that there are no jobs available, then they attribute this to their color. They are too sensitive and do not understand that there aren't enough jobs to go around."

"I heard some complaints against East Indians. They do not eat meat. They eat only vegetables. They are very slow in their work because they have no strength."

"The immigrants from India and Pakistan (including Bangladesh) are very dishonest. I read in the newspapers about the immigration racket they run in Canada. This makes it difficult to consider them for important positions."

The above are some of the characteristics that the informants attributed to the colored immigrants from India, Pakistan and Bangla Desh. The quotations indicate that there was a high degree of generalization and stereotyping and no endeavor has been made to distinguish the people in terms of level of ability, personality or character. The informants irrespective of first hand experience said or assumed that other people (employees, friends, clients or customers, labor union members) objected to colored people for these reasons. As a consequence of these assumptions, colored immigrants had been or were being considered by employers. If at all, only where no suitable white English or French personnel were available.

This stereotyping resulted in decisions made about colored immigrants as a group rather than as individuals. The results of this study indicate that the stereotype applies only to a part of the group. Thus, in contrast to the universal image of the occupationally unstable immigrant, more than half the sample had been in their present positions for more than three years. Though the stereotype of the occupationally unstable immigrant was developed on the basis of a sub-sample of transients, the generalized characteristics have been applied to all colored immigrants.

Other aspects of the stereotype may apply to a large number of the immigrants. For example, many of them in the sample earned their university degrees from their home countries, but, at the same time, a great many of them earned their degrees from Britain, the United States and Canada. Most of the sample who came to Canada are professional people. Strangely enough, those immigrants who had earned their degrees or diplomas from the Western countries had experienced the greatest discrimination. In such cases, the stereotype of the colored immigrant had often been imposed upon them when they were applying for jobs other than those for which the discriminators believed that colored immigrants were suited.

In so far as other personal characteristics are concerned, the research study does not provide any basis for confirming them. That statement that a large number of immigrants are dishonest and involved in immigration rackets, does not merit serious consideration, except in terms of the psychological state of the informant. Even if the claims were true of some immigrants it would be absurd to extend them to all colored peoples.

The beliefs about the occupational and personal characteristics of the immigrants were developed into stereotypes and thus show how the individual colored immigrant would be handicapped in applying for a job. The other important point was the way in which the employers attributed the unfavorable beliefs about colored immigrants' personal qualities to other people: white Canadian employees, friends and clients. This projection of one's own fears, beliefs and attitudes to other people proves that a great deal of discrimination practiced against colored immigrants was justified by the informants in terms of resistance or hostility of white people. It also indicates that colored people were rarely acceptable in positions of authority over white people. Thus, the colored man may be acceptable as a subordinate, particularly in a low status role, less acceptable as a colleague, and unacceptable as a superior.

The appraisals of the employers' statements or assessments about the occupational and personal qualities of the immigrants determine the general orientation of employers to the recruitment of colored immigrants. The basic approach was to employ colored immigrants for a job only when it was impossible to recruit and retain white people at an economic rate. Most of the employers interviewed said that no people from India, Pakistan or Bangla Desh applied for jobs in their organizations. An East Indian interviewed during our survey of immigrants applied for a job in that organization and was refused, but the job was advertised continuously in the newspaper for a long time.

An official of a large school board said that they used to hire teachers from Asian countries (includes India, Pakistan and Bangla Desh) but now the board policy is not to hire people from other countries. The official reiterated that even the people from India, Pakistan or Bangla Desh who come to Canada and get certified from the Department of Education are not hired. Those colored immigrants who obtained their teaching diplomas from Britain, the United States and Canada were also refused jobs because of unknown reasons. This policy of the school board virtually eliminated the chances of colored immigrants getting jobs in the public schools.

Another outcome of the interviews with the employers was that the colored people were taken only as 'a last resort' during periods of acute labor shortage. More over just because some employers had taken them on in the past, it did not mean that they were still accepting colored immigrants.

> "A few years ago there was a shortage of teachers, engineers and other professional people here and we took a number of people from other countries. Since there is a surplus of our own people in all trades we prefer to hire our people."

Many employers' preferences of white people and their reluctance to accept colored people for employment was quite simply a matter of 'justice'. Colored people were seen as an alien group, as outsiders and thus preference was given to 'their own kind of people'. They believed that if they take some colored people, it would open gates for a large number of them. This procedure for evaluating the colored applicant is that the employers see them first of all as a colored person and only secondly, if at all, in terms of his individual abilities and characteristics. It is the basis of much discrimination despite the formal declarations of many employers that they treated every applicant 'on his merits'. In some way or other they frequently assumed that all colored people had the same merits.

A large majority of employers said that their policy was to treat all employees and applicants equally and not to discriminate on the grounds of race or color. Some of the reactions of the employers are as follows:

"We do not tolerate discrimination based on race or color in our university."

"I assure you that there is no color discrimination in our firm."

Nevertheless, some of the employers said that the characteristics of some colored immigrants made it impossible to hire them for jobs:

"We follow the basic policy of equality in our organization. However, on some occasions, we can't employ a colored person despite his qualifications. The higher the level, the greater the pressure for not employing colored people."

The people who were interviewed in the survey were senior representatives of large plants, corporations or companies. Generally they had experience in employing people at senior, executive or administrative levels. As senior executives they were not aware of the way policy was implemented at lower levels and the problems associated with it here. Therefore, they were aware of the problems associated with employing colored people at executive level. At the time of the survey, no colored person was working at senior or executive levels in any of the organizations visited.

It was observed that there was a tendency among some employers who employed colored people to claim that they did not discriminate. It should be understood that because they employed colored people in the past did not mean they were still employing them. Most importantly, because colored people were employed in some types of jobs it did not follow that they were acceptable at all levels, in all functions in the organization nor did it imply that there was no discrimination in aspects of employment policy other than recruitment, such as promotion and training.

CHAPTER V

LABOR UNIONS

Representatives of labor unions--both local and national unions--were interviewed by the experts to elicit their opinions about the employment of colored people and their problems. A large number of unionists told the interviewers that unions oppose all forms of racial discrimination by Governments, employers and workers. Some union members said that:

> "According to the policies of the union, no discrimination in any form would be tolerated."

Despite the fair policies of the unions, the interviews with the representatives of the labor unions and the employers concluded that there is color discrimination on a smaller scale in the unions as well as in the employment of colored people.

The number of colored people who are members of labor unions is very small. Our survey of immigrants included questions on membership in the labor unions. The answers show that a large number of immigrants irrespective of membership in the unions suffered personal experiences of discrimination.

During our interviews with the unionists we found that some union officials do not tolerate discrimination and do take action against discriminators. By official action alone, they were not able to curb discrimination against colored immigrants.

Some unionists reluctantly agreed that there is some discrimination while employing colored people in large plants or firms on a personal basis only. They did investigate the complaints of the members of the union but they would not know anything about the colored applicants before obtaining employment.

Representatives of some unions said that there were cases, not very often, when a colored immigrant would seem to have a genuine grievance. But it was usually impossible to prove that discrimination had occurred:

> "If a colored person complains that he has been wrongly fired, after looking at the situation, we may feel that he is right. But, in many

instances, the union is powerless because it is very difficult to prove it. If the employers say that the colored man is not a good worker and the supervisor or his superior supports him, we can't be sure of proving anything because it is not possible to show that discrimination occurred."

A number of labor unions are exclusively dominated either by French Canadians or by English Canadians. On several occasions, the representatives of unions dominated by the English Canadians said that French Canadians discriminate against colored people and vice versa. One unionist responded:

"There are a number of nonwhites working in the companies and they belong to our union. They have the same rights, privileges and responsibilities as the other members. Since the union believes in socialistic ideas we treat all the members equally in a democratic way.

"Instead of receiving complaints from colored people we receive complaints from French Canadians. They say that colored people come to Canada and take their jobs away from them. They do not like colored people coming over here."

One French Canadian official commented:

"As you know higher positions are taken over by the English. They do not like colored, French Canadians and other minorities. English people discriminate against colored people but not French Canadians because they are a minority in Canada."

The outcome of the interviews with the local employers and unionists shed light on the reasons why employers were reluctant to take colored people as apprentices: they expected resistance from union members. One official puts it this way:

"In our plant shop stewards screen and recommend people for jobs. In that process if a shop steward does not like colored people or any other group, he does not recommend them for jobs."

"In our plant most of the employees are French speaking. Whenever there is a job opening the employees bring their friends or relatives for jobs here. We never received any inquiries from colored people for jobs."

White members of the unions considered colored immigrants as alien groups who do not share the culture, values or norms of either French or English groups. They were considered as inadequate union members in terms of allegiance and participation in union activities.

> "The colored people do not participate in union activities. They pay their dues and then disappear. It may be due to the newness of the country and also they may be afraid to tell their grievances because they think they may lose their jobs."

> "They do not have any commitment to the labor union movement. They never show up for meetings. They join the union because they think it is a protection against losing their jobs."

The "foreignness" of colored immigrants was also the basis of discrimination by union members. This characteristic combined with the occupational and personal characteristics attributed to colored immigrants produce hostility and resistance to them from white members.

To implement the policies of the unions, union officials needed the support of the rank-and-file members and their superiors. In many instances they could not always be certain of the support of the white members in opposing cases of discrimination; quite the contrary.

CHAPTER VI

MANPOWER AND IMMIGRATION CENTERS

The officials of Manpower and Immigration Centers were interviewed to elicit their opinions with regard to the employment of colored immigrants. The main themes emerged from these interviews: first, there is discrimination, to a smaller extent, in employing colored and they were unable to stop discrimination completely; secondly, since they sympathize with reasons why employers refused colored people, they tended to minimize the extent of discrimination purely on grounds of race or color.

Sixty-five per cent of the immigrants interviewed had used the services of the federal and provincial Manpower Centers the last time they had been looking for a job; six per cent had gotten their current job through the Manpower Centers. A significant number of the immigrants used the facilities of Manpower Centers. Only eighteen per cent of the immigrants who used the services of the Manpower Centers said that they found the centers useful in obtaining some kind of employment.

Since many colored immigrants go to the Manpower Centers to get help, the researcher felt it essential to get the views of the people associated with the employment of colored immigrants. The Manpower officials who were interviewed expressed that colored immigrants pose problems for them, which arise partly from the characteristics of the immigrants and partly from the reluctance of employers to accept them.

The inference of the Manpower officials as to the characteristics of the immigrants was similar to that of employers, labor unionists and employment exchanges. They too indicated the problems of immigrants relating to language, indigenous qualifications and instability in staying in one job. They mentioned that if immigrants have problems with languages--the English and the French languages--they send them to their special language centers run by the provincial government. The selected immigrants who attend the language classes are paid by the government till they complete their courses in either languages. Successful completion of courses does not guarantee employment. A large number of immigrants attend the government language centers (COFI) so that they could have some form of income to support themselves.

The officials of Manpower Centers said that the manual and semi-skilled workers are more likely to get some form of employment in comparison to those who have professional qualifications. They expressed, however, that immigrants from India, Pakistan and Bangla Desh are considered as better qualified than other colored immigrants.

According to the regulations of Manpower and Immigration Department, if any employers refuse a person employment because of applicant's race or color, the centers would report him to the government. Legal action could be taken against such employers. This means that any employers that may discriminate are not likely to do so in such a way as to be apparent to the Manpower Centers. Under such circumstances, the officials may take a passive attitude towards the whole situation.

Some of the official responses are as follows:

We very rarely hear complaints from the applicants about discrimination. I am frank in telling you that there is discrimination to a small extent. Manpower cannot remedy the situation of discrimination because employers would say that there is no position open. I give you an instance: one employer told an east Indian that there are enough number of colored people in the plant and he does not like to hire any more colored. When we tried to check this, he immediately replied "there is no job available here." In such cases, the Manpower counselors can't do a thing.

Another official replied:

We have no way of knowing and taking action. The employers are very smart. They can always give some wild reasons for not hiring. They are the final authority in hiring people.

Manpower officials mentioned that employers never openly refuse to take colored people for jobs but in many cases where an employer refused a colored person work it is for some good reasons and has nothing whatsoever to do with discrimination based on color or race. A large number of them felt that it would be absurd to assume that every refusal constitutes an act of discrimination.

The results of the survey of the immigrants and the interviews with employers indicated that the degree of discrimination was likely to be no less for the more qualified than it was for the manual as well as semi-skilled workers.

CHAPTER VII

HOUSING OF COLORED PEOPLE

The place where one lives is important for the happiness and well being of an individual. Several questions were asked to find out how satisfied the colored immigrants were with regard to housing because very often any difficulties related to housing are connected with prejudice or discrimination. Discrimination in housing was limited to a small number of colored immigrants from India, Pakistan and Bangla Desh.

Those immigrants who complained about housing difficulties mentioned discrimination as one aspect of many problems they face in Canada. Some of them mentioned that they were not able to obtain housing in certain areas due to their color or national origin and imposed constraints on their range of choice in housing.

In the survey of the immigrants only four per cent owned or jointly shared the dwellings; the remaining 96 per cent were in some type of rented accommodation.

In this chapter, we look into the types of houses the immigrants live in and the variety of problems they face in searching for suitable living accommodation. We include the results of our experiences with the landlords, estate agents and the explanations they gave for their behavior towards colored immigrants.

A series of field tests were carried out in connection with discrimination in housing. In this connection, a white Canadian and a colored immigrant applied for accommodation from landlords and they assumed the same type of professional roles with equivalent levels of income (the white Canadian was a school teacher and the colored person was also a school teacher). In some other cases, the white Canadian and the colored person adopted manual worker roles. The same testers went to the estate agents and housing offices. Forty landlords were approached in person and eighty by telephone.

The colored person was discriminated against one twelfth of the time when he contacted the landlords. The white Canadian met no discrimination whatsoever.

The landlords were chosen through newspaper advertisements and from 'to let' boards outside the housing offices. The colored person was offered the accommodations on the same terms as the white Canadian thirty-five times. Only five times did the colored person face some form of discrimination.

Table 14

Personal Contacts With Landlords (40 contacts)

Number of times discrimination occurred	5
Number of times both applicants were given equal opportunity	35
Total contacts:	40
Types of Discrimination (Five Times)	
Colored person was told that the place was taken but white Canadian was told that the place was available	3
Colored person was asked for higher rent then the white Canadian	2
Total:	5

Subtle discrimination exists in cases where the colored person was told that the place was taken when in fact it was vacant. In one case the custodian told the colored tester "no place for niggers here". But a significant number of times (35 times out of 40) the responses of the landlords were the same for both applicants.

The following table indicates the results of telephone inquiries to landlords (see Table 15, page 53).

When the landlords were called on the telephone for accommodation, they asked the applicants to come down and have a look at the place. When the applicants--both the colored and the white--went to see the landlords personally, ten out of eighty times the colored person was discriminated against.

The results of the above findings indicate the extent of discrimination in housing much lower than in employment but still existent. One interesting fact is that the incidences of discrimination varied according to the role assumed by the

-52-

Table 15

Findings of Telephone Inquiries to Landlords

(80 Telephone Inquiries)

Number of times discrimination occurred	10
Number of times discrimination did not occur	70
Total inquiries:	80
Types of Discrimination (10 Times)	
Colored person was told that the place was taken	6
Colored person was asked higher rent whereas white Canadian was asked to pay less	4
Total cases:	10

tester. If the colored person assumed a higher position he was treated a little better. There was a change in the attitudes of the landlords when they came to know the status of his job. In our interviews with the landlords, we asked them to give the reasons for refusing accommodation to the colored people. Some of the explanations of the landlords are given below:

"Colored people do not take care of their places and some times skip the place without paying their rent."

"Many colored people live in a small place."

"We don't have any colored people living in our buildings."

"They are not very clean."

Our interviews with the landlords indicate that discrimination exists in housing on a limited scale.

Later in the survey we contacted ten estate agents and ten housing offices, through our testers, to determine the nature and extent of discrimination in housing. They were also interviewed for further clarification on housing of the colored people.

The results of the tests are given in Table 16, page 54, and Table 17, page 54.

Table 16

Results of the Tests With Estate Agents (Ten Contacts)

Number of times discrimination occurred	0
Number of times both applicants were treated equally	<u>10</u>
	10

Table 17

Results of Tests With Housing Offices (Ten Contacts)

Number of times discrimination occurred		2
Number of times both of them treated equally		<u>8</u>
	Total	10

<u>Types of Discrimination</u>

Colored person was told no places are available; white Canadian was told that places are available	2

Even though the degree of the incidence of discrimination is small, at least a small number of colored people suffered discrimination.

Interviews were conducted with the officials of estate agents and housing offices to learn the reasons for discrimination in housing. Some of the responses are given below:

> We have no problem in placing colored people. Once in a while, some landlords do not like to have them for various reasons. Some of them are: do not have any colored people in this place, they cannot afford to pay rent, etc. But such cases of refusal are very small.

> If a person has money and a good job we don't care whether he is white, black or brown. Sometimes colored people can't afford to pay the rent and thus housing is refused.

Only once we had a little trouble in placing a colored couple. The neighborhood is completely English and the landlord did not like to have any colored people in that place. Since we are in business we had to search elsewhere for another place.

If a colored person moves into a neighborhood then more colored people move in. After some time the whole area becomes colored. We have to worry about the property values.

The responses of the officials show that problems in finding places for colored people in particular areas were infrequent. Some white people object to having colored people as their neighbors. Landlords felt that colored people are not good tenants in paying rent or keeping the place clean.

The statements made by estate agents, housing officials and landlords show that race or color was being used to discriminate against colored people irrespective of their qualifications. The criterion used by them to evaluate colored people was skin color rather than other characteristics. Those situations where discrimination occurred were when colored immigrants appeared in person for housing.

Several questions were asked in questionnaire-interviews with the immigrants to find out the proportion who claimed experiences of discrimination based on their beliefs whether their beliefs were based on personal experience or other people's experience. The following table gives the findings of the questions.

Table 18

Claims of Discrimination in Housing

Number of informants:	East Indian 32 %	Pakistanis & Bangladeshis 14 %
Personal experience of discrimination claimed and evidence produced	18	5
Personal experience of discrimination claimed and no evidence produced	14	3
Belief in discrimination through the experiences of others only	13	22
Applied only where they are acceptable	28	25
Belief in discrimination among others--avoided it through special characteristics or luck	12	27

Continued

Table 18 Continued

	East Indian	Pakistanis & Bangladeshis
Number of Informants:	32	14
	%	%
Don't know--no reasons given for the existence of discrimination, not sure about source of belief in discrimination	<u>15</u>	<u>18</u>
Total	100	100

The findings show that a large number of colored immigrants believed in the existence of discrimination in housing and many of them avoided it by applying to the landlords who would accept colored people. In many instances they lived with their friends and relatives and thus protected themselves from even awareness of discrimination.

In short, discrimination in housing, on a limited scale, exists and it was revealed both by the tests and interviews with landlords, estate agents and housing officials.

SUMMARY AND CONCLUSIONS

The research study was designed to find out whether racial discrimination exists in Canada; if so, how extensive is it. We used three surveys in the study as instruments for research: in the first survey, questionnaire-interviews were conducted among colored immigrants to find out about their life in Canada; in the second survey, personal interviews were conducted among the potential discriminators to find out the attitudes of the employers towards colored people as a group and how they justified their behavior; in the third survey, field tests were undertaken to find out whether the claims of discrimination by colored people were based on factual information or their own imagination.

After a careful study of several aspects of life in Canada--such as employment, housing and other related services--we came to the conclusion that racial discrimination varied from one job level to another and from low status to high status. Based on our tests the experiences of white and colored testers the physical characteristics such as skin color, facial appearance, texture of hair, were the major components responsible for discrimination. In some cases, religion was also a main factor associated with discrimination in jobs and housing.

People coming from Asia were the victims of racial discrimination in Canada. They felt the pain of discrimination, mostly in the areas of employment and housing. The outcome of the personal interviews with the employers suggested that colored immigrants are different from white immigrants in their culture and outlook on life. Some of the employers view all colored immigrants alike and others make distinctions based on their physical characteristics and educational qualifications. Many Asians were found working in professional areas but there was a trend to replace them as soon as white persons were available to occupy those positions.

The findings of the three surveys--the personal interviews with colored immigrants, personal interviews with potential discriminators, and field tests--

indicate beyond a shadow of doubt that racial discrimination exists in Canada and also give us the opinions of the people who are in a position to discriminate and the field tests to substantiate the claims of discrimination by colored people. The main objective of the study has never been to blame any group of people; instead it discovers the problems of colored people who have been treated differently in Canadian society because of their color or racial origin. It also delves into the effects of discrimination or the feelings and ways of life of colored people.

It is interesting to explore the intentions of the people who are in a position to discriminate against colored people and in the ways in which they justify their actions. The surveys we have conducted would give the intentions and justifications for differential treatment of colored people by the discriminators. Firstly, there are some white employers who reject all colored people as a group and would give no reasons for their actions; secondly, some white people give different reasons for discrimination against colored people; a third group of white people vehemently deny any type of discrimination practiced by them and conceal their real feelings towards colored people. Lastly, some white employers did not like to be interviewed for the survey. Those employers who took part in the interviews gave various reasons or justifications for their treatment of colored people differently from white people. Some of them said that while they would accept colored people, others would not accept them for employment; fellow employers, white employees, tenants, landlords and neighbors. Here is was not clear whether the person was projecting his own feelings or using this as an excuse to justify his own actions.

It was found that some employers had experienced resistance from white employees in hiring colored people but as long as the number was kept at a very low level the resistance was kept at a minimum. In some capacities--salesman, bank tellers, supervisors, etc.--where the contacts were with the public or the white subordinates, colored people were not usually preferred. A few years ago when there was a grave shortage of professionals--especially in teaching and technical areas--colored people along with other white immigrants were hired to fill the positions. At present there is a surplus of professionals in these areas, in consequence, colored people meet more discrimination than the white immigrants.

Discrimination against colored people exists in housing but the extent of discrimination is minimal.

Some employers in the surveys expressed their doubts about the qualifications of the colored people who were applying for jobs. They tried to justify their actions against colored people by stating that they were less qualified and less able than white people for jobs to which they aspired. They also mentioned that they come to Canada with indigenous degrees and thus do not meet the standards of Canadian educational institutions and work standards. Even if we agree with this statement, we have to look at those colored people who have earned their degrees from advanced countries of the west, especially from Canada, the United States, Britain and Germany. The most able and best qualified people, ie., people who have earned their degrees from advanced countries of the west, had experienced discrimination on a wider scale. Those people who have been in Canada for a longer time and who have tried to move away from the roles prescribed for them, by aspiring to get better jobs, have exposed themselves much more frequently to the possibility of discrimination.

Another element waited for the colored immigrants when looking for employment in Canada. Many employers politely refused to consider them for employment by telling them flatly that they have "no Canadian experience". After a mild persuasion, some employers told us that "Canadian experience" meant lack of familiarity with Canadian culture and Canadian social institutions. This inability of colored applicants to be familiar with Canadian culture and customs occurred because they arrived in Canada quite recently. In this way, color becomes all the more important in considering them for employment than the qualifications required for a job.

The question of "Canadian experience" in rejecting jobs for colored people becomes important in the future because the children born to colored people in Canada attend Canadian educational institutions and thus possess the same characteristics as a white born Canadian, except color of the skin. Conversely, many of the handicaps possessed by their parents (being a colored immigrant from a foreign culture) are lacking in their children and they demand equal rights and privileges as a white person in Canadian society. This new generation of colored people who are growing up in Canada would face the same problems as their parents because the stereotype of an inferior colored person would continue to be projected by whites on to them.

In a limited number of cases, the employers were justified to reject the applications of colored people based on their qualifications and experience to be effective in a particular kind of job. But, in many cases, the employers and the landlords created a generalized image of colored person as inferior and less able, based on the characteristics of the less able, without taking into account the individual differences of the immigrants. This type of stereotyping of colored immigrants led to injustice. This unique situation was brought out in the discussions with employers, Manpower and Immigration officials and labor unionists. Under such circumstances, a well qualified colored person would never get a chance of consideration for employment with people who are in a position to discriminate.

Employers argue that colored people have more job mobility and thus add a risk of high turnover to the employers. According to the findings of our surveys, colored people had less mobility than attributed by the employers. Some mobility is caused by the immigrant taking a low paying job initially until he finds suitable employment in his areas of specialization.

In the course of our surveys we came across another type of discrimination practiced against colored immigrants. Some employers hire only a limited number of colored people and then refuse to take any more. For instance, staff of the Manpower and Immigration department sent a colored person for a job interview. When the colored person was seen he was told that the company has enough colored people and does not like to hire any more. The colored person who was rejected because the determined number had been filled was justified in claiming that he is being rejected because of color or national origin.

After analyzing the findings of the three surveys and the impact of discrimination on the colored people's feelings, we came to the conclusion that discrimination has a bad effect on their feelings and ways of life in Canada. They faced discrimination in the hands of employers and landlords and the hostility of the white people with whom they come in contact made their lives disappointing in Canada. These factors, among others, made them believe that there is color discrimination against them practiced by white people. The worst part of it was that it was more subtle and painful than that in operation in many other countries, ie. United States, Britain, Australia, South Africa. Many times they were not even aware that they were discriminated against in jobs and housing unless some one who knows the real situation told them.

In not too distant future, colored people would make up their own social class in Canadian society because the practice of discrimination forces them to form their own social groups or enclaves where they find belongingness and solace.

The interviews with white employers revealed that colored people are discriminated against in jobs by employers or their white employees or customers or both. This means that colored people are taken on only when white people are not available to fill the jobs. Colored people secure jobs only due to the forces of circumstances, not because they are qualified to occupy the positions.

APPENDIX

Classification of Immigrants' Occupation

	%
Unskilled Manual	0.0
Skilled Manual	11.0
Non-manual	53.0
Unemployed/retired/at school	15.0
Work at school/college/university	<u>21.0</u>
	100.0

Head of Household

Man	96%
Woman	<u>4%</u>
	100%

Marital Status of Immigrants

Married (includes separated)	66.0%
Not married (includes single, widowed, divorced)	33.0
No answer	<u>1.0</u>
	100.0%

Proficiency in Spoken English

Fluent speaking and understanding	66.0%
Fairly good speaking, very good understanding	29.0
Fairly good speaking and understanding	4.0
Understands simple questions, speaks a few sentences	<u>1.0</u>
	100.0%

Educational Qualifications of the Immigrants

Secondary School	7.0%
Teacher's College	2.0
University	80.0
Technical College	<u>11.0</u>
	100.0%

Age Group of the Immigrants

16-24 years	6.0%
25-34	50.0
35-44	40.0
45-54	3.0
55-64	1.0
65 and over	0.0
	100.0%

Length of time in Canada and Claims of Personal Discrimination

6 months or less	9%
7-12 months	12
Over 1 year--up to 3 years	19
Over 3 years	7
	47%

Note: Totals do not add up to 100 per cent because only personal experience of discrimination is added.

Details of the Surveys on Potential Discriminators

Employment:
      6 - Public employers
      10 - Commercial Organizations (both manufacturing and retail chains)

Local Employers:
      30 - Local employers who include:
           5 - Manufacturers
          20 - Retail outlets
           5 - Service companies

Labor Unions:
      10 - Labor Unions include:
          National, regional and local representatives

Employment Agencies: 10

    Selected at random from the classified telephone directory.

Manpower and Immigration Offices:

    5 - they were selected at different places in Montreal

Accommodation:

    Estate agents and local housing offices were selected from local classified directory, companies advertised in the local press and room or apartment to let boards outside the buildings.

Banks:
    5 - Leading Banks in Montreal

Details of the Field Tests

The following gives particular details of the field tests. In our field tests in each area (housing, employment, commercial services), first a colored immigrant (East India, Pakistani or Bangladeshi), then a white Canadian would apply for what seemed to be available to all people irrespective of color or ethnic origin. In each test the testers would have equivalent occupational qualifications and requirements.

Housing Tests

1. Landlords - 120 contacts
    a. 40 contacts in person
    b. 80 contacts by telephone
2. Estate Agents - ten contacts
3. Housing offices - ten contacts

In the tests each tester assumed two roles: one professional role and the other working class. First tests were carried out on a sample of firms or organizations which have been named as having discrimination in the survey of immigrants.

Employment Tests

Twenty-four tests were conducted in the areas of employment on different firms and organizations.

The Questionnaire-Interviews for the Immigrants

All Informants   Code   Column

Q. 1a) In what country were you born?

	India	1
	Bangla Desh	2
	Pakistan (West)	3
	Other (state) _____	4
	Office use only	5

b) In what month and year did you come to Canada?

	Before 1960	1
	1960-1963	2
	1964-June 1966	3
	July 1966-Dec. 1968	4
	1969-1970	5
	Other _____	6
	Office use	7

c) How does life in Canada compare with what you thought it would be like--it is better, about the same or worse than you expected?

	Better	1
	About same	2
	Worse	3
	Mixed feelings	4
	No answer	5

d) Give your expectations as an arriving immigrant, what elements in Canadian life have come as a pleasant surprise.

	Economic	1
	Social	2
	Occupational	3
	Educational	4
	Religious	5
	None	6

e) Given your expectations as an arriving immigrant, what elements in Canadian life have disappointed you.

	Economic	1
	Social	2
	Occupational	3
	Educational	4
	Religious	5

If He Gives More Information (Write Out in Full)

_____
_____
_____

All Informants

		Code	Column
Q. 2a) In the three months before you came to Canada, did you have a regular job?	Yes No (b)	1 2	

If 'yes' ask questions (i) - (vii) with regard to job in India/Pakistan/Bangla Desh. Record in first column of the table below.

		Code	Column
b) Are you working at the moment?	Yes No	4 5	

If 'No'

		Code	Column
c) When did you last have regular employment in Canada?	Less than 1 month ago 1-3 months ago 4-6 months ago 7-12 months ago Over 1 year ago Never in Canada	1 2 3 4 5 6	

If working at the moment ask questions (i) - (vii) about present job: record in second column of the table below.

If not working at the moment ask questions (i) - (vii) about last regular employment in Canada: record in second column of the table below.

If have never had regular employment in Canada skip to question number 3a.

Q. 2 (continued)

		Q. 2a Job in country of Origin	Q. b/c Present/Last Employment in Canada
i) Industry?			
ii) Position?			
iii) How long employed?	6 months or less	1	1
	7-12 months	2	2
	Over 1, up to 3 years	3	3
	Over 3 years	4	4
iv) How was job obtained:	Informal contacts	1	1
	Direct application	2	2
	Advertisement	3	3
	Employment Agency	4	4
	Direct recruitment	5	5
	Other _____	6	6
v) How happy are/were with your employers?	Very happy	1	1
	Reasonably happy	2	2
	Not very happy	3	3
	Very unhappy	4	4
vi) How happy are/were you with your fellow workers?	Very happy	1	1
	Reasonably happy	2	2
	Not very happy	3	3
	Very unhappy	4	4
vii) What prospects of promotion do/did you feel you have/had?	Very good prospects	1	1
	Fair prospects	2	2
	Little prospects	3	3
	No prospects	4	4

All Informants   Code   Column

Q. 3a) Do you believe that there are any
       employers in Canada who would   Yes   1
       refuse a person a job just because   No (Q.4)   2
       of his race or color, rather than   Not sure (Q.4)   3
       for some other reason?

   If 'Yes' ask questions b-d   95 or more   1
                                               85-94   2
   b) Out of every hundred employers in   45-84   3
      Canada how many would you guess   20-44   4
      discriminate against colored (India/   1-19   5
      Pakistan/ Bangla Desh) immigrants   None   6
      when employing them?   Don't know   7

   c) How certain are you that there is   Positive   1
      discrimination by employers?   Very certain   2
                                               Fairly certain   3
                                               Not certain at all 4

   d) Is your view based on personal   Personal experience 5
      experience, on what you have been   Personal experience
      told by other people, or both per-   and other   6
      sonal experience and other people?   Other people only(f) 7
                                               Don't know (f)   8

   If personal experience (Codes 6 or 7)

   e) Will you please give me details of the personal experience that
      makes you feel there is discrimination in employment?

   ⎧ Probe for full list of personal experience and record on a separate ⎫
   ⎨ sheet. Record one experience on each sheet, up to a maximum of   ⎬
   ⎩ two for any one informant.   ⎭

If Views Are Based on Other People Only or Don't Know - Q.3(d) Coded

f) In your view, is there any reason why people you know have experienced discrimination when seeking employment, but you have not?
   WRITE OUT_____

Question 3c) - <u>Description of Refusal of Work Because of Race or Color</u>
(Obtain as much detail as possible, and cover all
relevant sections)

i) Name of firm/institution _____ type of firm: public ☐ 1
   _____   private ☐ 2
   _____
   _____ approximate no.
                             of employees: _____.

ii) How did informant make application?
_____
_____

iii) For what type of work?
_____
_____

iv) Who did informant see?
_____
_____

v) What evidence does person have that it was refused because of race or color?
(PROBE)
_____
_____
_____

If Evidence is Not Direct Statement of Color by Employer (PROBE)

vi) How he knows it was not given to some one with better experience/skills?
_____
_____

vii) How he knows there was a vacancy to be filled?
_____
_____

viii) That the vacancy was still there?
_____

ix) Other evidence for knowing it was because of color or race:
_____
_____

Q. 3. x) Have you ever been refused membership in a labor union/professional organization?

        Yes ☐ 1   No ☐ 2   Never applied ☐ 3

If yes,

Why does person believe it was refused? (Probe)

_____

_____

Q. 4a) Have you ever applied for a job at an employer where you had no idea whether they employed people from India/Pakistan/Bangla Desh?

        Have applied for a job at an employer with no idea whether they employed immigrants   1

OR

Have you only applied for jobs where you know discrimination did not occur?

        Have only applied for jobs where it was known discrimination did not occur   2

        Don't know   3

If 'Have only applied for jobs where discrimination known not to occur':

b) How did you know there was no discrimination?

WRITE IN _____

_____

_____

All Informants

Q. 5a) When you were last looking for a job did you try to: Never looked for a job in Canada 1

    i) use the local Manpower and Immigration Department?

If Yes

b) How useful did you find it?)
)
If 'very useful' or 'useful') RECORD BELOW
)
c) In what way?)
)
If 'not very useful' or 'useless') RECORD BELOW
)
d) In what way?)

Repeat a-d for: ii) answer advertisements)
iii) approach employers direct) RECORD BELOW

	(i) Manpower and Immigration Department	(ii) Advertisements	(iii) Employers direct
a) Yes	1	1	1
No	2	2	2
Office use	3	3	3
IF YES			
b) Very useful	4	4	4
Useful	5	5	5
Not very useful	6	6	6
Useless	7	7	7
Can't say	8	8	8

IF 'VERY USEFUL' or 'USEFUL

c) In what way WRITE OUT _____

IF 'NOT VERY USEFUL' or
  'USELESS'

d) In what way? WRITE OUT _____

All Informants

Q.6 Do you own the place where you now live or do you rent it?

Owned or being bought solely	1
Rented and furnished	2
Rented and unfurnished	3
Other (state)_____	4

Q. 7a) How satisfied are you with the accommodation?

Very satisfied	1
Satisfied	2
Uncertain, don't know	3
Dissatisfied	4
Very dissatisfied	5

If 'Dissatisfied' or 'Very Dissatisfied' ask b) and c)

b) What is wrong with it? write it.

_____

_____

c) Why do you think that you were given this type of accommodation? Write out. If Discrimination or Prejudice Mentioned Probe for Details.

_____

_____

_____

_____

All Informants

Q. 8) In the long term what sort of accommodation would you most like to get - to buy a house or apartment, or a privately rented property?

Purchase	1
Private renting	2
Don't know	3

Q. 9a) Have you ever tried to get a mortgage or borrow money from a bank or a loan company?

Yes	1
No (Q.10)	2

If 'Yes' (Code 1 RNGED)

b) Have you been refused a mortgage or loan?

Yes	3
No (d)	4

If 'Yes' (Code 3 Ringed)

Why do you think it was refused?

_____

_____

IF DISCRIMINATION OR PREJUDICE MENTIONED, WRITE IT ON A SEPARATE SHEET.

<u>If 'No' at Q. 9b</u>

    d) Was there anything about the loan which you   Yes   1
        feel was any different from the loan which   No (Q. 10)   2
        a white Canadian would get?   Don't know (Q.10)   3

<u>If 'Yes' at Q. 9d</u>

    e) How was it different?

    _____

    _____

    _____

Q. 9c - Refusal of Mortgage or Loan   Code   Col.

  i) Name of organization: Year of application

    _____   _____

 ii) Reasons why refused

    _____

iii) Evidence that it was due to color or race?

    _____

    _____

 iv) If evidence is <u>not direct statement of color race</u> by organization

    _____

    _____

  v) Other evidence that it was color rather than other reasons.

    _____

    _____

    _____

    _____

Q. 10a) Do you think that there are any landlords
        in Canada who would refuse a person an   Yes   1
        apartment, house or rooms purely because   No (f)   2
        of race or color?   Not sure (f)   3

If 'Yes'

    b) Is this based on personal experience what you have been told by other people or both personal experience and other people?

    Personal experience   4
    Personal experience and others   5
    Other people only (e)   6
    Don't know (e)   7

If 'Personal Experience' (b coded 4 or 5)

    c) How many times have you been refused accommodation because of race or color? WRITE IN_____.

    d) Please will you give me details of the occasion when you were most sure it was because of race or color?

RECORD FULL DETAILS ON ANOTHER SHEET OF PAPER

People Whose Views Based on 'Other People Only' or "Don't Know" (Q. 10b coded 6 or 7)

e) In your view is there any reason why people you know have experienced discrimination when seeking accommodation, but you have not? Write Out.

_____

_____

_____

If 'No' or 'Not Sure' That Landlords Would Refuse (Q. 10a coded 2 or 3)

    f) Have you ever applied for a house, apartment or rooms from a white landlord who was a complete stranger?

    Yes   1
    No   2

Q. 10d - Description of Grounds for Claiming That Accommodation was Refused Because of Prejudice or Discrimination

  i) Details of accommodation applied for

_____

_____

ii) What evidence does the person have that refusal was the result of discrimination or prejudice because of color or race?

_____
_____
_____

iii) Comments of landlord/agent

_____
_____
_____
_____

All Informants

Q. 11) Here is a list - SHOW LIST - of different services. Would you tell me:

    a) Which of these, if any, do you think that Indian/Pakistani/Bangladeshi immigrants have any problems within Canada? (Code in column below.)

    FOR EACH ITEM MENTIONED ASK

    b) What sort of problems do you think immigrants have with_____?

    c) Do you know this from personal experience or from other people, or both?

IF 'Personal Experience' or 'Both' (Q.c coded 1 or 3) Record Details on Another Sheet of Paper.

Services	(a) Present problems	(b) Type of problems presented	(c) Own experiences	Others experiences	Both	Don't Know	Q.12 Used/obtained
Hire Purchase	1		1	2	3	4	1
Car Insurance	2		1	2	3	4	2
Hotel/Motel accommodation	3		1	2	3	4	3
Holiday accommodation	4		1	2	3	4	4
Places of entertainment	5		1	2	3	4	5
None of these	0			None of these			0

Q. 12) Would you tell me which of these you personally have used or obtained in Canada?

Q. 11 (c) Details of Problems With Regard to List of Services Because of Race or Color (Record Details Under Appropriate Heading)

i) Hire Purchase _____

_____

_____

ii) Car Insurance _____

_____

_____

iii) Hotel/Motel Accommodation _____

_____

_____

iv) Place of Entertainment _____

_____

All Informants   Code Col.

Q. 13a) In your view has it become easier or more difficult for a person from India/Pakistan/Bangla Desh to live in Canada, or hasn't it changed?	Easier	1
	No change	2
	More difficult	3
	Don't know	4

If 'Easier' or 'More Difficult'

b) What has made it like that? WRITE IN

_____

_____

_____

All Informants   Code Col.

Q. 14a) Would you say that there is any kind   Yes   1
         of color discrimination in Canada today?   No   2
                                                         Don't know   3

   Unless 'Don't Know'

   b) What makes you say that? WRITE IN

   _____

   _____

   _____

Classification Data (a)

A. How old were you when you left school?   10-12   1
                                                        13-15   2
                                                        16-18   3
                                                        19-21   4

B. What type of school or college/university   Primary school   1
   did you last attend?   Secondary school 2
                                                        Teachers college 3
                                                        University   4
                                                        Technical school 5
                                                        Other(state)____ 6

C. Did you pass any public examination?   Yes   1
                                                        No   2
                                                        Other   3

   If 'Yes' - which?

   _____

   _____

D. Do you have any (other) certificates or   Yes   1
   qualifications?   No   2

   If 'Yes' - which?
   Certificates _____

   _____
   Other qualifications _____

   _____

-78-

E. What language (s) did you speak as a child?   at home? _____ 1
                                                          _____ 2
                                                 at school? _____ 1
                                                            _____ 2

F. Estimate of informant's spoken English.
   Fluent speaking & understanding   1
   Fairly good speaking, very good
      understanding   2
   Fairly good speaking, under-
      standing   3
   Understands simple questions,
      speaks a few words   4
   Nil   0

Classification Data (b)

	Code Col.		Code Col.
Age Group: 16-24	1	Occupation of Informant	
25-34	2		
35-44	3	_____	
45-54	4	_____	
55-64	5	Industry of Informant	
65-	6		
		_____	
		_____	
Sex:		Classification of Informant's Occupation	
Man - Head of household	7		
Woman - Head of household	8		
		Unskilled manual	1
		Skilled manual	2
Marital Status:		Non-manual	3
Married (includes separated)	1	Unemployed/retired	4
Not married (includes single, widowed, divorced)	2	At school/college	5
		Informant is:	
Working:		Member of professional organization	6
Full time (30 plus hours)	1	Member of labor union	7
Part time (under 30 hours)	2	Don't know	8
Not working	3		
Composition of Household:		Name of Union _____	
No. of adults 2 plus _____		Nationality of Employer	
No. of children 3 plus _____			
No. of children 1-2 _____			
Total _____		_____	

Day (ring) M1 T2 W3 Th4 F5 S6 Su7

Date_____

I DECLARE THAT THIS QUESTIONNAIRE-INTERVIEW HAS BEEN CONDUCTED ACCORDING TO THE DIRECTIONS AND HAS BEEN EDITED.

Signed_____

Name of the Informant_____

Local Address_____

Telephone Number_____

DAVID GLENN HUNT
MEMORIAL LIBRARY
GALVESTON COLLEGE